Glory

B!

1000 Miles of Mishaps and Miracles

Dave Graham

LIGHTSMITH PUBLISHERS
Thorne Bay, Alaska

Copyright © 2020 by Dave Graham

All rights reserved. No part of this publication may be reproduced, distributed or transmitted in any form or by any means, including photocopying, recording, or other electronic or mechanical methods, without the prior written permission of the publisher, except in the case of brief quotations embodied in critical reviews and certain other noncommercial uses permitted by copyright law. For permission requests, write to the publisher, addressed "Attention: Permissions Coordinator," at the address below.

Lightsmith Publishers
P.O. Box 19293
Thorne Bay, AK 99919
www.LightsmithPublishers.com

Ordering Information:
Quantity sales. Special discounts are available on quantity purchases by corporations, associations, and others. For details, contact the "Special Sales Department" at the address above. Lightsmith Publishers is an imprint of the Wilderness School Institute, a nonprofit educational organization that offers outdoor youth activities in wilderness settings, including training in wilderness skills and nature studies, as well as the publication of curriculum on related subjects, through the Wilderness School Press, and their children's imprint Summers Island Press.

Glory B! 1000 Miles of Mishaps and Miracles/ Dave Graham

ISBN: 978-1-944798-31-4

/Paperback edition

To my children, for all the times they asked why.

Contents

Part I
Liberty Bay to Friday Harbor

1. How Did That Happen?
2. Is This All There Is?
3. Can We Really Do It?
4. Glory B!

Part II
Pender Island to Campbell River

5. Getting Underway
6. Dead in the Water
7. Casting Off All Lines
8. Man Overboard!
9. Night in a Ghost Town
10. A Series of Divine Appointments

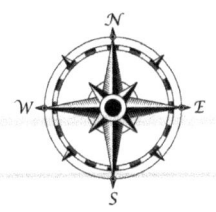

Part III
Campbell River to Port Hardy

11 **Narrow Places**
12 The Hardest Thing
13 Big Trouble
14 Into The Wilderness

Part IV
Safety Cove to Thorne Bay

15 Crossing Over

16 Island Life

17 To See The Dream

A Word to Readers

About the Author

LOG OF THE GLORY B.

Liberty Bay to Friday Harbor

2013

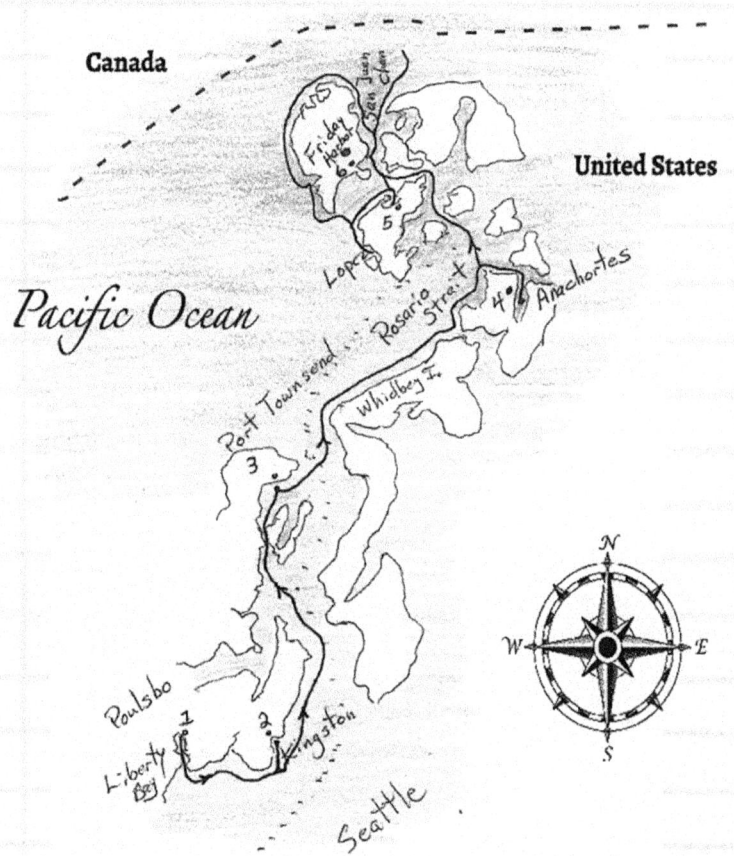

Part One

Liberty Bay to Friday Harbor

51° N   128° W

1   How Did That Happen?

I'm not going to tell Lilly what I'm seeing up here, she had dropped below to make tea. I had goofed. We were not where we were supposed to be. Now, the weather was kicking up and the waves were breaking over the port side. The Queen Charlotte Sound was pushing us hard into the strait and it didn't look good. We had to make the cover of Calvert Island before dark or we'd be in big trouble.

Having spent the last weeks from Seattle to here, we had never been exposed to the big waters of the open ocean. Instead, we had been "gunk-holing" up the East coast of Vancouver Island, ducking into safe harbors early in the day, never being out after dark. As beginners, we had it easy. No worrying about difficult navigation: I would just measure thirty to forty miles on the chart, figure the compass setting to get there, and off we would go. All we had to do was stay on the course I had chosen, then—when ready to pull over—look for a small bay to turn into.

This was different.

What if we couldn't find a safe spot before dark?

Right now I couldn't even see the shore we left from this morning, it was just water with rocks sticking up everywhere. Last night when I was plotting our course I thought I had it all planned out. All I had to do was motor for thirty minutes after leaving the bay, turn right between two giant rocks, then turn west to three hundred and twenty degrees and stay on that heading all day until we hit Calvert Island.

What two big rocks? There were big rocks everywhere! They were all around us. What happened? I double checked my time.

There it was.

I hadn't been on this heading for thirty minutes, it had only been fifteen.

I had looked over at Lilly then, seated in her spot against the starboard rail. Her bright orange life jacket fastened up tight and tied off to the life line with the end of one of the sail ropes, a precaution she had been taking ever since falling overboard off Quadra Island. She was looking at the rocks with the same apprehension I was feeling myself.

"How about some tea?" I had asked her.

She unhooked and went down below, while I tried to take account of the situation.

I had left Port Hardy super early because I knew this was a long stretch of open water and I needed all the daylight I could get. Last night I had poured over the charts. Getting my dividers out, I measured several times the exact distance out of the marina to where I had to turn northwest. However, when I sighted the two big rocks I was sure that was the passageway I was looking for. These had to be the right ones. So off I went. After clearing them, I made my turn onto three hundred and twenty degrees.

Now, there were rocks everywhere.

I looked at the open ocean far to the West and I could see a ferry passing by in the distance. It was so small it looked like a toy boat on the horizon. I wondered why he was way over there when straight ahead was the entrance to the Fitz Hugh Sound and Calvert Island, the gateway to the protected Inside

Passage that went through Canada, all the way up to Alaska. Then it hit me, he was avoiding the rocks.

Now that I was out here I couldn't just head over to where the ferry was. It was miles out of my way and I wouldn't be able to make Calvert Island by dark. It was also where most of the rocks were. I compromised and went a little toward the ferry, mostly for Calvert Island.

What could I do—we were already out here—we would just have to watch out for the rocks.

When Lilly came back with two mugs of tea, I asked her to take the helm while I checked the bilge. On top of everything else, the shaft seal had been leaking more and more, and the bilge pump wasn't working right. I had intended to get a new one in Port Hardy but the prices were too high. We would be in civilization in a couple of days and could get one then. Which meant I would have to check the water level every hour to make sure it wasn't getting too high.

Uh-oh, there was already a lot of water in the bilge. The bilge pump showed a large amp draw but the water level wasn't going down. Apparently it was stuck. I would have to pump the bilge by hand. So, I dug out the guzzler hand bilge pump, stuck the discharge end over the rail and started pumping away. Fifty pumps should do it.

It took one hundred and fifty pumps.

Already the shaft leak was getting worse. I wondered if I could do a hundred and fifty pumps every hour.

"Lilly," I said as I climbed out of the hatchway, again, "I may need some help." I didn't want to make too much of a fuss over the leak. The problem was, how many disasters could my wife take? Could we take turns on the bilge pump? Then is when the seriousness of the situation hit. If my backup hand bilge pump would give out and we couldn't get help soon, the boat could actually sink out here.

How in the world did I get us into this situation?

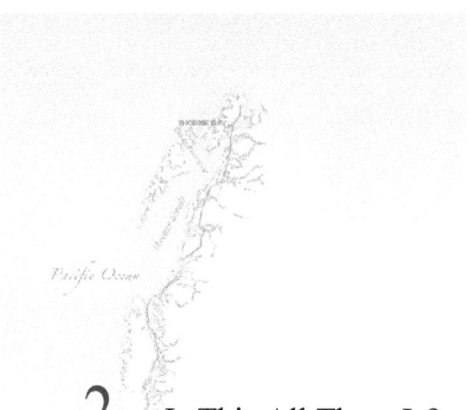

$35.8°N \quad 97.4°W$

2 Is This All There Is?

I've had this dream for a long time. Sailing up the Inside Passage to Alaska, past beautiful islands and wilderness places. Rugged mountains and the kinds of adventure you only read about. I had already been around the world twice, in the Navy, but it wasn't the same thing.

Whenever I did get liberty in all those exotic places I had dreamed about, I missed having someone I loved to share it with. It wasn't what I thought it would be. Still, there was something compelling about the ocean that drew me back to it again, and again. I would spend endless hours on the fantail just looking.

I found my lifetime companion, Lilly, right after getting out of the service. She also had an adventurous spirit and even loved boats. Her parents had been divorced and when she visited dad, he would take her out on the big ocean. From the young age of five years old they would get up early in the morning hook up to the little eight foot boat and head to the beach. Wait in endless lines at the pier to have their boat set in the water. Then head straight for the horizon, many times being out of sight of land. He even fell in once and had a tough time getting back in the boat. So, I had the perfect companion for real sailing: she was a dreamer like myself. She also had no real fear of the water.

We met at a Jesus meeting and were married three weeks later. I graduated from college and took my first teaching job in Las Vegas, Nevada. We were well on the way to middle class America when we purchased our first boat. It was a twenty-three foot, shoal draft sloop that we sailed back and forth across Lake Mead, with great pleasure. Our kids were so small that all of us, and the family dog, fit down below if I would chuck the dog out the hatch first thing in the morning.

When the kids were older and in their teens we lived for a year aboard a forty-three foot sloop along the coast of Oregon. We still occasionally dreamed of long term cruising, but by then the kids were involved with school, life was expensive, and dreams were put on the back burner.

Before I knew it, I was seventy years old and a lifetime had passed by.

Where had my life gone? Now, I had begun to slow down. I knew I had this love of nature and the outdoors, including the waters of the world. I also loved building. On our five acres, I had been building for over ten years, recently finishing Lilly's office and mine. I had barns, fences, workshop, as well as a chicken coop and goat pen.

I had just finished my own office, filled with the things important to me. Family pictures, pieces of nature I had collected, beautiful birds, and of course books. But now, the boat idea just seemed to jump up and grab me. If I didn't do it now, when would I? We were going to Colorado, this spring, to promote Lilly's new book, *Gold Trap*. That would be halfway to Seattle—where all the boats were.

Suddenly, it all seemed logical to me. We could rent out our house—buy a boat with that extra money—and we could be off. I talked to Lilly about the project and she seemed to be on board. But when I started carrying her books to store in the little cabin at the back of the property, she gave me a start.

Seeing me pass by with one of her favorite books, she said, "Where are you going with that book?"

I responded, "Where? To store it in the back cabin."

Lilly then replied, "Not that one!"

Red flag.

Had she not agreed with me that in two weeks we would be leaving for the gold mines of Colorado, and renting out the house? We would be driving the station wagon, packed with camping gear and whatever else we may need. I tried to be firm and demand no more than a dozen books to be taken. Reluctantly, she agreed, but every time I walked by her office with another pile of books, she would have to inspect the pile, herself, for any "important" ones. Her collection of books alone numbered over a thousand. This was not good. Soon I was moving books in the middle of the night so I didn't have to go through inspection.

We had raised three kids and had a lifetime of furniture, and memorabilia. All must be protected and could not be replaced. So, I started building huge wooden crates, screwing down the lids so mice could not enter. Meanwhile, the impossible conditions of this adventure crept in around the excitement. We were to take the rent money and travel throughout Colorado, then on to Seattle and purchase a cruising sailboat with just our rent money?

The reality of doing this thing hit me. The doubts started as I sat in my office and took time to slow down and think. Lilly and I had a nice spot here in Oklahoma. Five acres and our daughter living nearby, in her own house across the pasture. Between us we had barns, chickens, horses and goats. There was just enough money to make ends meet. No extras.

The short excursion we had planned for Lilly's book tour was originally going to be only a few weeks of camping and visiting relatives along the way. The idea definitely needed more thought. Maybe even a little prayer.

I started praying more. I had also been in the habit for years of collecting Bible verses on subjects I was praying about. In no time at all, I had a big stack on my desk of three by five cards related to my situation. I would read them over and over. They seemed so wild to me. Some said I could have whatever I could believe for. That was pretty far out.

I spent days collecting verses but nothing

seemed to be happening, I didn't feel any closer to God. Then a thought hit me like lightning: *"Just believe one."*

What did that mean?

If the Bible said it, I had to agree. But it seemed to me the believing part couldn't be proven until a person actually acted on it. So, that very day I wrote in my journal that I was officially asking God to bless this search for a sailboat that I had on my heart for so long. A "blue water" cruising sailboat that could go anywhere in the world.

I felt as long as I could do something in that direction I would be stepping out in faith. Is that how it works? It was a long way to Seattle, anything could happen along the way. And if anything did it would cost a lot more then one month's rent money to get fixed.

Any way I looked at it, the whole project seemed bigger each day. Lilly liked her country home and had been enjoying having her own office, with the perfect little deck to have coffee on while thinking and plotting out her books. I also began to realize that most people don't move into homes for only six months. The truth was, if we rented, it would probably need to be for at least a year. I couldn't see down the road that far at this point, but did I really have to? I could only see the next step. Could my faith really open doors with such a small beginning?

The way I looked at it, there was only one way to find out.

$47.6°N \quad 122.3°W$

3. Can We Really Do It?

It was rather surreal, hiding the boxes of books so Lilly wouldn't dig through them and really mess up my efforts to seal up the valuables. I had valuables also: my pair of stuffed wood ducks, one of the most beautiful of the water birds; my custom made cedar canoe that I had built; along with all the tools that a man needs to build and repair anything. I stood in the storage area surrounded by all that was important to Lilly and I. Was this dream I felt I had missed out on really worth all that we had built up in our lifetime?

But how would I even know if I didn't try?

I decided to go on.

We had purchased a new video camera to share with others our gold mine experiences to promote

Gold Trap, and possibly our coming sailing adventure. It was fun video taping ourselves on the road through Colorado gold mines and trying our hand at what was—to us—this new form of communication of posting brief film clips of our adventures on the Internet. However, we did everything we could think of in the gold fields in a mere two weeks. By that time, Lilly was already dreaming of her next book, and all I had on my mind was boats.

Once we decided to head to the coast, I couldn't get there fast enough. A real blessing was that one of our sons lived in the Seattle area. We decided to stay there and visit while we looked for a boat. From that point, we would be able to fan out all over the nearby coastal areas.

I remember having to tell people we liked their boat but had no money to purchase up front and would need to live on the boat while we paid for it. That got real old, real fast. It wasn't long before we realized it would take a miracle for anyone to go for that kind of a deal.

Within three weeks we had used up all of our traveling money for the month and would have to sit and wait for the coffers to fill up, again. By that time, we had discovered the small tourist town of Poulsbo, nearby. It had a marina and long boardwalk along Liberty Bay where we were drawn back to again, and again. The waterfront atmosphere was not only a great place to spend time, but there was always the hope that my constant prowling around the boats might turn up one I had overlooked before.

It was a splurge to go out for fish and chips but we both sensed we were finally up against reality itself. It seemed that no amount of religious mumble-jumbo could resist the real world we lived in. Was this where all our hopes and dreams would have to yield to what was real? As disappointing as it was, I didn't think anybody was going to sell us their boat if it was worth anything at all. Not on the terms we were stuck with. Today, I was tired of it.

Sitting at the tables outside, waiting for our lunch to be served, I could see a few of the closest boats in the marina. Suddenly, my eye caught something that I had not seen before. It was a boat, covered in cheap tarps, all shredded from months of winds. Maybe I had missed it earlier because it had been completely covered. Now, they had blown off to reveal the beautifully classic stern of a *Mariner:* the exact make and model of a boat I had dreamed about over thirty years before. No matter how old, they were still way outside of our price range.

Even so, I could hardly wait until after lunch, when we could walk the hundred yards to get a closer look. The area was gated so we could not get all the way out to the slip. But I figured out the slip number and went straight to the office. They would not say who owned the boat but promised to give them my phone number.

The following day, the owner called. I told him I loved his boat. Could I see it? He said the boat was not for sale but would be glad to show it to me. The appointment was in several days, and since I liked hanging around the boats, I actually saw him several times on the boat, in work clothes. He seemed busy cleaning up something, Probably the boat. When the day finally came and we walked up to the slip, I could see—sticking out from beneath the tattered blue tarps—the distinctive classic bowsprit, along with what I loved the most of this classic boat: a teak taffrail. Yes, it was covered with many months of moss and neglect but it was the real thing.

After a few minutes down below, I just wanted to take him to coffee so we could talk. Once sitting down, we chatted about his boat but he wasn't much of a talker. I tried to follow suit but we got nowhere. Finally, I just came straight to the point. I wanted his boat to take a trip up the Inside Passage, to Alaska: something I had dreamed about for many years.

Silence.

I told him his was the perfect boat I needed to do it in. While he didn't really comment about that, he didn't come right out and say, no. Instead, he told me he had a lot of the boat stuff in storage, if I wanted to see it. The statement caught me off guard.

"Sure I would love to see it," I said.

We made arrangements to meet the next week.

Back at the house, I told everyone, "I think this guy is going to sell to me!"

Next time I met with the man, we looked at the mass of sail and boat gear. I didn't look long. I wanted to tell him what a miracle this was: finding the exact boat my wife and I had picked out so long ago. To me, it was proof of my experiment that God could make things work out if we would but step out and have faith in Him. It was the kind of action He cared enough about—this stepping out—that literally caused God to work things out for us.

I got no answer for all that, but the man was definitely listening to me. So, I started to throw out numbers of what I felt it was worth. I said many of these boats were selling for at least twenty-thousand.

His reply floored me. "No, it isn't worth that much!"

I sensed that God was giving me favor and this boat was mine.

As we were walking back, we stopped to sit on a picnic bench. It was a good moment. I'm quite often not a listener but he finally said, "My wife and I have had dreams, too. But I've had a lot of bad luck and nothing good has happened for us since my heart attacks."

I couldn't help my enthusiastic reply. "Then we'll share our blessings with you."

The next time we got together, he seemed much more relaxed. We looked at the gear some more and talked boats a bit, but it was time to make a deal. I made my offer for ten thousand dollars, plus two thousand for him to carry the loan. The only thing he asked for was proof of income.

Knowing I was going to have to work for a while to pay it off, I had—only two days before—answered an ad and applied for a roofing job. Being in the huge metropolitan area of Seattle, I found myself one out of one hundred and fifty applicants. To my surprise, they hired me. At seventy, I had several trades with fifteen years of experience in each. But to me, this was another sign of God giving me favor. No mention was made of carrying roofing up three stories at my age. We signed the contract for the boat, and in six months it was paid for.

As a little side note, that roofing job ended when I made the last payment.

47.8° N   122.7° W

4 Glory B!

Lilly and I moved onto the boat immediately, walking on a cloud. The first big miracle had happened. Here we were with no money down, living on a boat we had picked out over thirty years ago. Working at a job that was less than a block from the boat, getting paid top dollar. Another little tidbit of encouragement, the slip fee was half price since it was a little narrower then the others.

Doing the roofing work took everything I had. I found that if I could take the pain of the first couple of weeks the body toughens up and it was very good for you. No pain no gain.

Our Mariner ketch (meaning it has two masts) was thirty-two feet long. It was big enough to live on

Glory B!

yet still small enough for Lilly and I to sail by ourselves. The weekends were great of course. I got to work on the dream. There was a thick layer of green moss over the entire taffrail. I just scraped it off and began sanding. The beautiful teak was just magic. Under all that moss was the most beautiful wood ever made by God. All I had to do was remove the dried-out outer layer, then oil the surface, and it looked like new.

The wooden masts were really beat up. They had been varnished years before and now starting to show big cracks of no varnish and water creeping into the wood and doing damage. There was even some soft punky wood at the base, a real indicator of serious rot. This is where my grandkids came in. What ten year old wouldn't like to climb a mast and sand it. I said I would pay him twenty dollars for each mast. But having to hang onto the sander and be thirty feet up in the air, dangling on a rope was just a few years ahead of him. He did one mast and we called it quits.

Down below was a whole different world. I loved the teak everywhere. The cute little kitchen and sink that you could have hot and cold water from shore power or foot pump. The hot water didn't work, which was disappointing since we had to live aboard. I started to realize how many things we take for granted.

Hot and cold running water were going to take a lot to get. I had to replace the water pump. Of course it was specially made for boats, so double the price. The hot water tank was broke and had to be replaced. We also started to be sensitive to space. Thirty two feet sounds and looks kind of big but the living area inside was merely fifteen of floor space with the engine room taking the last eight feet. The entire bow area was bunks and storage.

I do believe this is one of the charms for me, having everything needed in such a small place. The bathroom had a shower hose you could hook onto the faucet, with an on-off switch. The floor had a hole in it that drained the water into the bilge. The systems you can cram into a boat are just great. The woodwork was beautiful throughout but there were no cushions. Things like that deteriorate fast on a damp boat.

We waited till the last minute to do something about the cushions. When we finally decided to get under way, we ran to the nearest fabric store to get the foam. Actually, I checked a month earlier and the price of one hundred dollars per cushion had been over our head. Now we were desperate. Imagine our surprise when we got to the store and found that all foam was fifty percent off. Thank you, Lord, for yet another miracle.

The engine room and electrical system was disastrous. First thing noticeable was the floating oil in the bilge. Since the shaft seal was not dripping, where was the water coming from? Why wasn't the oil pan catching the drips? Maybe I should start with the simplest things. Like how to change the oil. What kind of oil—what viscosity? The only obvious thing was that it could only be done lying on my side, reaching around all sorts of hoses and pipes.

I didn't like crawling on my side in close places. But I took it the same way as any other distasteful—but necessary—thing that had to be done. Surprisingly, as I figured out the engine room and how everything worked, it became more appealing. There were two fuel filters side by side. I knew the fuel was probably in bad shape from condensation over the years, so, I purchased new ones. After that, I let a little fuel out of the tank at the bottom until I couldn't see any more rust chips coming out.

Next, one of the rubber hoses looked cracked, so

I replaced it. There was no sump pump hooked up properly. I purchased hoses and a new pump. All the through-hull valves (holes that let water in from the outside) seemed frozen open to whatever hoses and pipes they were connected to. Meaning I wouldn't be able to turn specific hoses off during an emergency and fix it. At the moment, though, I was afraid to get too rough with them and cause immediate leaks. So, I put that off until we could get the boat hauled out and on dry land at a boat yard..

It was March when we finally made the last payment. The trip to Alaska was becoming such a reality that we were referring to it as our "trip of a lifetime." Which had to be done in the summer months and was still some time away. A good thing, considering there was still a lot to do.

The bottom had to be scraped and painted and there were no electronics on the boat, only a compass. Having no experience with the newer electronics, I didn't realize the need for that simple four-hundred dollar tool: the chart-plotter. I knew we needed one of those but kept putting off the expensive purchase because I heard many people were simply downloading charts from the Internet and using an iPad for navigation. I did have an iPad.

Glory B!

At seventy, I had a difficult time relating to technical things. So, I talked to my son, who was a Coast Guard bosun, who told me what to do. It kind of went in one ear and out the other. However, I did have a fun time going through old charts from the used marine equipment stores. After six months of digging around in that great store, *Longship Marine* in Poulsbo, Washington, I got to know the owner, Aaron, very well. There seemed to be an endless list of things I might need on the boat; life jackets, fenders, books on what to do, replacement parts for everything, and of course an inflatable boat if ours should sink.

The money had long-since dried up but I knew we couldn't start on the trip without a dinghy. We found a great little racing boat about eight feet long, rather nice looking, with a small mast and sail. A perfect match for the classic lines of our boat. It would look good on the videos. I was surprised when Aaron interjected that it was a lousy choice for a dingy. But I bought it anyway.

The next thing on our list was getting some work done at the nearest boatyard in Port Townsend, some twenty miles away. Now would be a good time to go because the yard tends to be jammed in the summer.

We decided to head for Port Townsend and continue to fix things on the way. It would be our first sail.

My ignorance of even the rules of the waterways for small boats was the greatest of irritation to my Coast Guard son. He was very tactful and suggested a few trips around the area to get a feel for boating. So, we loaded up him, our daughter, and a couple of the grandkids, and off we went. It was worth everything we had gone through to see the smiles on the kid's faces when they took their turns at steering the boat.

The steering was pretty simple if you just stayed away from other boats. What was difficult was the moving water. We landlubbers are used to everything being under control. In this marine world, the street you are driving on is actually moving, even though you can't see it move most of the time. Being aware is a big deal. Not only the water but the air will push on you at the wrong moment and you will turn while the boat continues straight ahead. Very scary. But exciting if you enjoy that sort of thing. Which I did. We just needed a little more experience. The kind of experience we would get "out there." After all, like *Captain Ron* says, if anything goes wrong, we could just "...pull over and ask directions."

The shakedown cruise worked out so nicely, I couldn't see any reason why we shouldn't be able to handle the twenty-mile trip to the boatyard all by ourselves.

47.8° N   122.4° W
to
48.11° N   122.8° W

5 Getting Underway

This was it. Years of prayer and we were finally casting off the lines from the dock and motoring out of Liberty Bay. How exciting to experience the physical evidence of what we had been dreaming about for so long. Had it truly come from believing we could have whatever we say—or just some bizarre coincidence?

My friend Paul, who I worked with on the roofing job, took a picture of us gliding out of Liberty Bay for parts unknown. The chug, chug of the diesel in the background, as we passed his home on the bay, was music to my ears.

We went by the Navy base, then had narrow Agate Passage to go through after turning north. Going under the bridge to Bainbridge Island, we headed North through Port Madison with Seattle proper immediately to the east. All I had to do is keep the land on my port side. Apple Tree Cove—where we would spend the first night—was just an hour or so away. Lilly and I had agreed that we would begin our travels with short daylight hops, settle in early, and so eliminate a lot of errors that could occur after nightfall. Or when we were already tired from too long of a day at the helm.

Finally our first anchorage came into sight: the little coastal town of Kingston. Since we had no depth sounder I crowded us up as close to the entrance to the marina as possible. How could it be too shallow here? There were already other boats anchored close by. We had traveled about fifteen miles that day without mishap. Not much to brag about but we did it.

Early the next morning, while Lilly was busy finishing up some work she had committed to, I jumped into the dingy and went for coffee at the marina. I was excited to get on the way, so returned in an hour ready to get going. As I tried to climb back aboard I couldn't reach the life lines. It caught me off guard. What was going on? When I left I had no trouble getting into the dingy. Then it hit me.

We were running out of water under the boat.

At that very moment of awareness, the whole boat rolled away from me onto her port side. Thank God she hadn't rolled my way. Then I heard this blood curdling scream coming from below decks.

Lilly had been working away intently, seated on the port side settee, the side onto which it rolled. The horrible sound of masts and rigging all clanging together at once—then being thrown down the six feet to lay on her side—was more than she could take. She could see water covering the porthole and thought she was sinking.

It took me a few minutes to scramble up over the side and grab the life rail.

It wasn't until Lilly finally managed to make it up on deck—and see several kids playing in the water only up to their knees—that she realized she was in no danger of drowning. But I had made the biggest of mistakes. Scaring my wife on the first day out.

Everything was explainable. This once a year, super low tide would be gone in four hours, and the incoming tide would naturally float our boat, again. But that didn't matter at the moment. I had scared my sailing partner right off the bat, and there was still eight hundred miles to go. To top it off, we were in full view of the ferry dock, letting passengers on and off, a short distance across the cove.

After a few embarrassing hours, we finally got underway, again.

We cruised past such interesting places as Apple Cove Point, Point No Point, Skunk Bay and finally Oak Bay before coming up on the entrance to the narrow Port Townsend Canal. Being the novice I was—and since I had spent the morning on the port side of my beautiful boat—I approached my first canal transit with little confidence. It was a mile long and, thank God, I noticed a light buoy at the other end. All I had to do was line myself up, wait for the tide, and head in. No problems. After clearing the canal we passed Port Hadlock, motored for another hour, and finally came in sight of Port Townsend and its large busy marina.

There were about twenty boats at anchor outside the breakwater. This time, I tried to find the best spot. I decided on the outer edge of the group to anchor—plenty deep—and that way if I drifted I had room to correct myself without fouling someone else's anchor. From here, I would have to row quite a distance in the dinghy to get to the marina.

These waters that were at the edge of the giant

Strait of Juan de Fuca—the doorway to the mighty Pacific Ocean—felt different than the calm stillness of Liberty Bay. Sitting in the dinghy, the water seemed to be moving mostly up and down and the sides of our little craft were only six inches above all that big water. This ocean that I had been drawn to all my life felt like something alive that was literally pulling at me as I rowed. I had never felt so small and inconsequential before.

It took half an hour just to row all the way to the docks. When I tied up and walked over to the busy boatyard to make an appointment, it turned out there was a two-day wait before we could even get the boat hauled out. We settled down to the long wait.

The next day, my son came to see how we were doing. I jumped into the dingy and went to the marina to pick him up. On our way back he grabbed the oars. The dingy took everything he had to row, paddling against that strong current. We didn't seem to be gaining much headway. The waves were almost over the gunnels. It felt like forever until we made it to the boat.

We tied the dinghy alongside, and went down below to visit. When I happened to look out the porthole a while later, it suddenly seemed that every boat in the harbor was drifting by us at the same time. I leapt to the hatch and stuck my head out.

I was the one racing out to sea!

We were dragging our anchor. I started the engine immediately, thanking God that there had been no other boats close enough to run into. After that scare, I decided to pay the twenty dollar overnight fee and took the *Glory B* over to the guest dock. My son gave us a few much needed tips on setting the anchor in various types of sea-bottom. I had enough of these rip roaring tides.

When I woke the following morning, I could see the fuel dock from where we were tied up. Already there was a long line of boats waiting for gas. I wasn't interested in fighting the crowds by trying to maneuver my boat in such tight quarters. So I just grabbed the gas can and rowed the dingy over to the pumps. The gal that was pumping was very busy and finally filled up my gas can, gave me a receipt and went on to another customer. I didn't catch the fact that the attendant gave me regular gas instead of diesel.

I paddled back to the boat and poured it in. For some reason, I looked at the receipt. When I saw that I had bought gas and not diesel, my heart sank.

Quickly, I headed back to the pumps, where the attendant explained that because I handed over a red five gallon container—which was the color for regular gasoline—they had filled it with that. I should have given her a yellow container.

I had heard of terrible things that could happen to a diesel engine by putting regular gas in it. I walked the few hundred yards to a diesel repair shop and told them my situation. They said that a diesel engine could take a ten percent gas mix. I pulled the boat over to the pumps and filled it with all the diesel I could get into the tank, and we headed back to the anchorage area.

This time, when we went to anchor, I remembered the advice from the day before. Drop the anchor, go in reverse until you could feel the effect of it digging in, and the anchor was set. It is also best to put out five times as much rode (or rope) as the water you are in. I didn't look forward to having to paddle the dinghy back and forth from this far out, but there was little I could do about that at this time. However—even after all those precautions—we woke the next morning only to discover we were dragging the anchor, yet again.

Enough was enough.

Glory B!

We decided to head north to Anacortes. I wasn't sure if I could get the work done there, but I knew it would at least be a beautiful protected bay behind Guemes Island, and not at the doorway of this turbulent Strait of Juan de Fuca.

Anacortes, which was situated on beautiful Fidalgo Island, was the first community we settled in when coming to the Northwest over thirty-five years ago. But before we could get there, we would have to cross the international shipping lanes going in to Seattle, one of the busiest marine highways in the U.S. Lilly seemed worried about it, but I knew it was less than a mile across from here. How could it be a problem? What are the chances of having trouble in that amount of space?

The tankers were just huge. They were like a city block full of high-rise buildings bearing down on us. They caused a backwash of swells two to three feet high that made our little ketch rock back and forth. Banging and clashing Lilly's dishes down below. We crossed the southbound lane with no problems. In a few minutes, we would be clear of all those huge things. I could see another one coming farther off but I had no worries.

Out of habit, I glanced down to check the oil

gauge. Forty pounds was normal. It was at zero. Was I seeing things? I took a second look. Absolutely no oil pressure. None. I pushed the throttle lever forward to neutral and jumped down below to take a look at what was going on.

One of the hoses had burst and oil was spraying out everywhere!

I raced back into the cockpit to pull the kill button. That would stop the engine immediately but we would then be dead in the water: the worst situation any boat could be in, and one that could be deadly in the middle of a shipping lane. The big ships can't stop—or even turn quickly—in that narrow channel. Especially on sudden notice.

Lilly knew what was up. Instantly, she was standing in front of the kill button. "We just need to get a little farther, we're still in the shipping channel and that next one is coming too fast!"

In over forty years of marriage I had never been physical with Lilly. But she had no idea what we were really up against, and I didn't have time to explain.

48.5° N   122.6° W
to
48.5°N   123° W

6   Dead in the Water

I didn't do what my first reaction was and just shove Lilly aside. I stopped and, yes, there was something she could do: raise the sails, even though there is absolutely no wind. I turned the engine off and dived down below, leaving Lilly at the helm in case a puff of wind came up and she could steer the *Glory B* toward shore and out of harm's way. I didn't feel any wind at the moment but it gave her something to focus on rather than panic.

The oil had stopped squirting once I turned the engine off. I found some special tape I had tucked away for just this kind of problem. It was super tough and sticky. As I wound it around the oily hose, several turns, it began to stick to itself. Soon the dripping stopped. Just in case, I wound the rest of the tape until it was gone, then poured in the backup oil I brought along and jumped back up into the cockpit.

To my surprise I felt a slight breeze. She had been praying and there seemed to be just enough wind to inch us toward shore and out of danger. After that, the motor started immediately and we resumed our course. In just a few minutes the tanker went by. I'm sure the pilot had no idea what that little boat was doing so close to them. To this day, Lilly says it was an answer from God to her most desperate prayer; that little puff of air that seemed so important at the moment.

I didn't even try to clean up the mess. It could wait until Anacortes.

Under way, again, we had the pleasure of seeing the Whidbey Island Air-Force base up close as we passed by. Actually, I think we may have been in a restricted area. After that, we passed one of the prettiest bridges in Washington. Deception Pass bridge had beautiful arches for support but they were hundreds of feet into the air. I would love to sail under that bridge someday, with it's swirling currents underneath.

Fidalgo Island came up next. It was one of the favorite spots for Lilly and I. The real gateway to the

San Juan Islands that we had been pressed to go to many years ago. On the south of it was beautiful Deception pass, called that because Captain Vancouver thought it was a pass to the East side of the Island but it turned out it was but a big bay.

Keeping Fidalgo on my starboard side, I turned east into the pass between Fidalgo and Guemes Island, finally dropping anchor in Fidalgo Bay. It was a perfectly protected bay, but I put out extra anchor line any way. I was starting to get the point of why good sailors were always taking precautions for something most of us landlubbers could not think of.

By that time Lilly needed a few days rest and this was a good place for it.

My own projects would take several days since the oil was everywhere. These were things I did not look forward to but had to deal with. The bilge seemed always full of water. The bilge pump was a horrible thing to work on. Covered in a black coating of oil, even if you had gloves on it still spread throughout the boat. I would clean up all the oil I could see but what was left in the bilge never seemed to go away.

There was also a small leak at the packing gland, where the shaft went outside the boat. It was a very fancy seal. The old style I was used to was a piece of braided rope pushed against the shaft to make it bulge and make a tight seal. If it leaked you just tightened the packing a little more. This new ceramic seal was two flat surfaces polished and pushed together with a little water to lubricate it. Which would have to be repaired; one more thing that had to wait until the boat was hauled out.

One afternoon, my son called and asked if we needed company. He showed up half an hour later in his Coast Guard boat. He dropped anchor close by so I jumped in the dingy and rowed over. He handed over a bag that contained four quarts of oil and a little cash. He didn't say much—he was obviously on the job—but it was nice to know he was thinking of us.

Meanwhile back on the *Glory B*, Lilly was writing away furiously. She knew there would be no internet in Canada and she had deadlines to keep. We decided to take a few extra days so I could clean things up and she could write. Between chores, we took a few walks around the town and even met a friend of years ago. Finally we were ready to head for Friday Harbor—this was the kind of sailing I had dreamed of for years—the San Juan Islands. We pulled up anchor with no problems, tied it to the deck and headed out of Fidalgo Bay. In a few minutes, we were navigating through Guemes Channel between Guemes and Whidbey Island. Past the ferry terminal and on our way west.

We couldn't head directly for Friday Harbor, since Lopez Island was in the way so we sailed through Rosario Straits, that body of water that moved from north to south separating, the mainland to the east and the San Juans to the west. It was less than ten miles wide, maybe thirty miles long, but was the connection to the turbulent Strait of Juan de Fuca to the south and the Strait of Georgia in the north. The Strait of Juan de Fuca being the path from the North Pacific Ocean. We were fortunate the weather was mild and beautiful. These Pacific Northwest islands had green pines over rocky hills that came right down to the water. Weaving in and out of such beauty was breath taking. I had felt the same way many years ago when we first came here and it was wonderful to be back.

It was easy to recognize little Blakely to the north and Decatur Island to the south, pass between the two of them, then make our big turn to almost three hundred and sixty degrees to get around the top of Lopez Island. We went past Swift Bay, Shoal Bay, and the very northern tip of Lopez. After that we went south far enough so I could do the two hundred and seventy degrees I needed to make Friday Harbor.

Now, we were finally able to do some real sailing. In no time we had the main pulled up and drawing good wind on the starboard tack. The air was light so I got out the one hundred and ten percent jib and off we went. It was only five or six miles to Friday Harbor. Being at the peak of the summer season, the harbor was so crowded we saw that we would have to drop anchor in an exposed part of the bay. But at least we were in Friday Harbor.

This had been the community we originally wanted to go to thirty years, ago. But so did everyone else back then. Job openings were few and far between. I had to take a job in Anacortes and wait for an opening in Friday Harbor. Surprisingly, we didn't have to wait long. Six months after arriving, we received a call from a Friday Harbor Christian school. Would we come to the island and take over the school? The main teacher had broken her arm and they needed a long-term substitute.

It was truly a time of miracles. The former teacher lived on a beautiful farm in the country and next to her was a vacant ten acre farm. We were able to rent it for two hundred dollars a month. We were overcome with how perfect the place was. The three kids soon had horses to ride and miles of country to roam in. So began many months of paradise. All the memories of those years flooded Lilly and I as we, once again, walked the familiar streets.

Back in the present world, we had a lot to do to get ready for crossing the Canadian border. We had purchased a kerosene stove in Liberty Bay. From day one it had a leak. At the time, I was very busy trying to get the boat ready for sail and the smell was put to the back burner. What was showing up is that all the tough projects were put off until the yard and we never went to the yard.

Now, here I was less than fifty miles from the Canadian border, in June, and still had a bilge that flooded only when the boat was moving; a pump that seemed to be letting water into the bilge rather than pumping it out; and a kerosene stove that smelled up the entire boat, so that wherever we went in town people stare at us.

But slowly everything eventually started to come together. I was able to order a new bilge pump from Seattle, and bought a new battery. Then we decided to go for a test run to see if I had fixed the flooding bilge. Less than a mile out, the bilge was flooding, again, and we had to turn back.

I worked more on the exhaust line of the bilge pump and made the loop higher, being so new at this sailing I didn't realize that when the boat leaned over the exhaust port would be below the waterline and so the bilge would fill up. I raised the loop of the pump even farther. Now, there would be no chance of water running back into boat. As an extra precaution I even installed a shut off valve. With that closed, I could be sure no water would be coming from that line.

I felt everything was repaired but was not going to head for Canada until we had made a good test run. We decided to go around the island. It would be a great trip in waters that had much history for Lilly and me.

So, on the busy Independence weekend holiday, we headed for the north end of the island. There was a resort called Roche Harbor that dominated that entire end. Established in 1886, it later became a famous vacation getaway for John Wayne during his movie career. We remembered it as the most stunningly beautiful part of the Island and had many pleasant hikes there on the beaches and in the woods. Now that we had the most perfect boat to explore in, we were looking forward to seeing some of the inlets and water ways, as well.

A lot had changed over the last thirty years. We found it full of boats, and hundreds of people walking the streets. An entire village had sprung up along the waterfront with shops, restaurants, and vacation homes. This was the busiest weekend of their entire the year. But for a couple who had wanted to get away from the crowds and hustle and into wilderness places, this was not for us.

So where do we go from here?

A conversation with a neighboring boater revealed there were many quiet spots to drop anchor in, a short distance away on the Mosquito Pass. Willing to bear the mosquitos rather than the crowds we left Roche Harbor behind and finally settled down. The place was much more to our liking. We later learned that it had not been named for the dreaded insects but for a fleet of small steam ships that serviced the entire waterway from Seattle to Skagway, for nearly a hundred years. While dangerous, because their boilers seemed to be always blowing up and burning the vessel to the waterline, the "Mosquito Fleet" was critical for getting goods and services to people in the isolated island communities.

After the development of the government-run marine highway system they were pushed out of business. We didn't know it then but the next piece of our original dream was falling into place. Much later we were to discover that the very place we anchored in was Nelson Cove. Named after a distant fisherman relative of mine who came here from Denmark over a hundred years ago. I had a fleeting thought that I might be following in the footsteps of destiny.

We woke up the next morning rested and ready to resume our circumnavigation and return to Friday Harbor. At this point we were halfway around the ten mile long San Juan Island, and it had been without disaster. Things were looking up. Coming out of Mosquito Pass we turned into the Haro Straits and headed south to where it merged with the Strait of Juan De Fuca.

There were kayakers enjoying the great weather, traveling as a group. Since we had no real wind we were under power. Soon it became obvious they were actually traveling faster then we were. But we were in no hurry. This is the island that had blessed us so much, years ago, and we would soon be off the southern tip, where our little farm had been, and the beach where the kids would ride their horses. Now we were enjoying a close look of the West side of the island, the side that had all the wildlife since it faced the big waters off the Strait of Juan de Fuca.

The hump back whales were here, going north, and we were very close. There was a Save-the-Whale group boat scurrying up and down the coast, trying to keep other boats away from the whales so as not to over stress them. They came close enough alongside of the *Glory B* to pass a note over to us on a long pole. What was this? A young woman hollered over that we should be much farther outboard of the whales.

Which we did not want to do considering our reluctance to be too far from the shore while we were testing our repair work. We would be turning north in a few miles and we trusted the whales to be much more adept at staying clear of us, than we of them. Besides that, we were coming up on, the famous Cattle Point Lighthouse; a well-known rough spot where the three bodies of water converged.

This is where the pleasures of the day's sail

diminished. Before we knew it, the tide was changing, the wind kicked up, and we were soon plowing into choppy seas. The kind Lilly did not enjoy. To reduce the bouncing I headed into the chop coming from the south. It helped but it wasn't getting us back to Friday Harbor. Meanwhile, the dingy was dragging and bouncing precariously off the stern and—because we had never faced waves this big before—I was concerned. If it flipped over I would not be able to right it fast enough and we would lose it.

Normally, we would have found a little cove to drop anchor in at this point, and wait things out. Our experiences had begun to teach us that the seas in this area tended to be calm in the mornings and kick up more in late afternoon and evenings. But there were no little coves near the wide rocky point of the island that hung down into these tumultuous waters. Now, we would have to venture quite a distance into them just to get safely around the rocky shore.

The conditions were getting worse by the minute and we were already reaching our limits. Looking closer, I could see the south end of Lopez across the channel and could just make out some kind of residence that might indicate a cove just north of it.

Glory B!

I was pretty sure we could make that spot before dark... but to do it we would have to turn crosswise to the mounting waves and head directly over.

from the

Photo Album...

LOG OF THE GLORY B.

Liberty Bay to Friday Harbor
145 Nautical Miles

Thinking back at seventy...is this all there is?

Did she have one more voyage left in her? More importantly, did we have one more left in us?

Leaving Liberty Bay...our first day of living the dream.

"We needed the Journey. To become someone different than we were—to break free from the things that held us back."

Hard aground the second day out. It's never as easy as it looks.

"There's always another reason to quit but if we don't try, we'll never know. Let's just see how far we can get..."

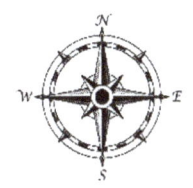

Our visit from the cavalry.

Going against the current has taken on a whole new meaning for me.

Lilly looking out at Shark Reef, where we spent the night with sea lions.

Mmm... Homemade bread from our galley.

Plotting my course to Canada. It's now, or never.

LOG OF THE GLORY B.

Pender Island to Campbell River

2014

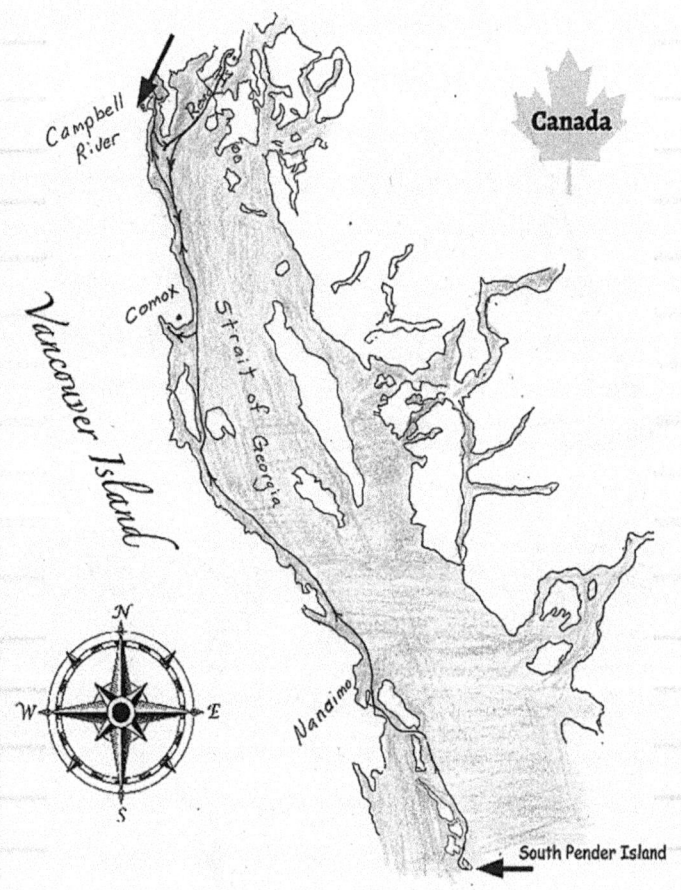

Part Two
Pender Island to Campbell River

48.5° N   122.9° W
to
48.8° N   123.3° W
to
49.2° N   123.9° W

7   Casting Off All Lines

Like most frightening things, they look a lot worse from a distance than they do going through them. This incident was no different. The boat was bouncing, waves were splashing over the bow, and sometimes the nose was literally dipping into them. Because we were no longer heading directly into the waves so we could go up and over, there was an exaggerated sense of rocking back and forth on our beam ends at the same time. All of which was very frightening for Lilly, who had never experienced anything like this.

On the other hand, this held no comparison to my Navy days' memories of hanging onto a steam wheel in the engine room of a huge ship in a stormy North Atlantic. Weather in which it was common to be in the middle of a ladder and suddenly find yourself at the top during one of those unexpected drops as she plowed over giant waves. Back then, there had even been a few that were strong enough to break windows out of the pilot house forty feet above decks. I knew from those experiences of having the ship roll so far that it was sucking air instead of water from the bottom—and could still right itself without sinking—that this amazing little sailboat could probably take a complete roll over and come up, again. But I would rather not have my wife get off at the next dock we tied up to and not ever want to get back on.

This became an obvious challenge for me throughout the entire voyage, in that our individual responses to circumstances were drastically different. It wasn't that we thought so differently, it was more because each of our past experiences were so vastly different from the other. But how do you deal with things like that? I had all I could do dealing with the moment at hand.

What seemed like a long time but was probably less than an hour, we finally crept into the cove on Lopez Island side of the straight, in the dark, looking for a safe enough spot just to drop anchor. By that time, we were exhausted and more than grateful for the comfort our little "home on the water" offered down below. Living in one's own familiar environment while traveling is one of the true beauties of the sailing life.

When we woke the next morning, all was as calm as we expected, and wildlife was everywhere. Really everywhere. There were hundreds of giant sea lions perched on rocks all around us, making loud barking sounds. They seemed to be saying who are these people? They don't belong here.

And we shouldn't have been there. We had come in on a high tide, last night, and now it was so low we were sitting in a pond with rocks sticking up everywhere. It took a lot of careful maneuvering, with Lilly up on the bow as we had to inch around huge boulders with groups of these creatures only a few feet away from us.

As we finally came out of the bay and entered the San Juan Channel, the beautiful quiet of the morning was such a contrast to yesterday's wild ride. To top it off a huge sea lion came up out of the water right beside us with a twenty pound salmon in its mouth. It was a moment we would never forget.

We continued up the coast on the east side of the channel and within a couple hours, we came to

Fisherman's Bay. It was a very unique entrance. You actually made a complete u-turn coming into the bay so that it was perfectly protected from the weather in the big San Juan Channel. After our choppy anchoring in Friday Harbor this was pleasant indeed. There was a cute little town along the waterfront with the backdrop of the snow-capped top of Mount Baker behind it that could be seen way on the mainland. We decided to take some time to look around, spend the night here, and head for Canada in the morning.

The next day, with a good deal of excited anticipation, we headed out. We approached the tight u-turn from the bay, and suddenly, several loud bangs came out of the motor. Now, what?

I immediately turned it off and looked around. In our favor, the tide was coming into the bay instead of going out. So, we floated backward—away from other traffic—so I could investigate. I found nothing wrong and tried to start the engine, again. It wouldn't even turn over. I decided we better go back to our old anchor spot.

We could find no mechanic to look at it, and after a few days, made an uneducated guess that the heads must be bad. I would have to do the repairs to go on

Glory B!

and by the time I had it all done, it would be too late in the summer to make the long passage. We would have to put off our plans of adventuring up the Inside Passage until next spring.

A decision that could have been much more disappointing if Lopez Island hadn't turned out to be the most pleasant place we had ever been. The town was only a short walk away, with an excellent library and grocery store within reach. Considering the marina included resort privileges of swimming pool, gym, and hot tub, we felt more like we had landed in the lap of luxury than being stranded. All for less money than we had been paying for a slip back in Pouslbo. We began to feel the Lord's blessing upon us in so many ways.

We attended the little Island Church, nearby, and made many good friendships over the weeks that have continued well past our stay there. The bookstore began to carry Lilly's books and she joined the local writers group which met regularly at the library. She enjoyed the pleasant atmosphere and adopted a favorite corner to work in every day while I worked on the engine and many of those other small repairs I had been putting off for so long.

Our time passed quickly in such comfortable

surroundings and before we knew it, our day of departure finally rolled around and we were off adventuring, again. At zero nine hundred we waved goodbye to our new island friends and aimed the *Glory B* north. After a brief stop at Friday Harbor, it wasn't long before we found ourselves just hours away from the border that had eluded us for over a year.

We still hadn't purchased that expensive chart plotter, but had acquired a secondary Delorme system. Mostly used as an emergency device, it did have a GPS dot that showed where we were on the screen. The only problem was that it had up to a half hour delay. If I watched it to let me know where I was, it would be up to two or three miles behind me. A fact I didn't realize until later. The only way I could use it for plotting was to have it give me a location every fifteen minutes. Another little thing we missed that turned out to be hugely expensive.

My thoughts were that in Canada chart plotters would be cheaper then U.S.. So I would get my dividers out and measure a fifty mile area and find some place to pull over for the night. Things are deceptive on the water. It's difficult to see whether there is a bay there or not. You have to get real close

Glory B!

to the land to tell. This is a little difficult because close to land is where the rocks are. Most of the time a thousand yards was good enough. My son, the bosun, would get very irritated at that approach. He would tell us, "The land is not your friend. Going into port is the most dangerous time. Deep water is good."

It was a beautiful day for sailing and by the early afternoon we were already pulling into Pender Island. There were two really isolated islands on the way out from Friday Harbor, Waldron Island on my starboard side and Stuart Island on the port side. As long as I kept Stuart Island to the West and I kept a tack of three hundred and thirty degrees I should hit the bay just right. Amazingly after a few hours there was the entrance to the bay just ahead and a park area was on the starboard side. We pulled over as close as possible to find something that looked like an official government check in place.

It turned out to be a phone booth.

The instructions were to call the number posted. A women asked questions of how many aboard, identification, the boat number, and how long are you going to stay? Within a few minutes we had an official number and permission to travel through

Canada. It felt a little anti-climatic after all the hours I had read the info on the internet and stared at the maps. Even though the park was very nice and it was mid summer there seemed to be no one there. It was during the week but to have such nice spots so close to the city, sounded great.

The next day we pulled away from the dock and headed north again. We would be on the west side of the Pender Islands and so in Swanson channel, to the East was Plumper Sound. That three-hundred and twenty degree number kept popping up. That's the compass setting for most of the trip. It was a clear day but a lot of islands all around us so we had to be on our toes and look for rocks and landmarks since we were navigating completely by compass and dead reckoning. We were just using the paper charts we had purchased back at the starting point, Liberty Bay, but they seemed very adequate. In an hour we had steered around the southeastern tip of Prevost Island and were in the big channel for this area, Trincomali Channel.

In the states we are so used to being crowded. If you like quiet, Canada is the place for you. I have always been a nature lover and this was the place for wildlife. It was the little things that I enjoyed the most. The quiet spot after an afternoon of chugging along. We sailed very little because if there was wind it was right on the nose and we would have to tack endlessly. But the six knots, sometimes slower if the tide was against us, was perfect for a man and his wife who were well past middle age. Just to sit and be part of that beautiful country, was worth whatever the cost.

It would not take long to be out of the Southern Gulf Islands. On reflection it is sad we did not look around a bit more. The anchoring spots were ideal. There were thousands of little bays to drop anchor in.

Late in the afternoon we would be entering our first narrows. The tides of Canada were extreme. The narrows were just wild. Fifteen knots of water moving, depending on coming or going, through these passes. Our first passage would be a place called Dodd Narrows. We were lucky and pulled up to the place within half an hour the tide was pulling us through the narrows. This is a perfect example of how you fuss and worry about things, thinking of all the negatives, and when you finally get there, it is hardly anything at all. Something that gave us more courage to go on.

Nanaimo was the next community on our map. It

looked very commercial, with lots of smoke and ocean tankers. It was about here that we got a little more confidence and realized we didn't need a town to anchor by. The best spots were the farthest from the towns. We anchored in a little bay called Departure Bay and were off early in the morning. On reflection, I wish we would have slowed down and smelled the roses a bit more. But we had so many disasters up until then I felt as if we were still fighting just to stay afloat.

By the next day, we were starting to catch our breath, and beginning to enjoy just cruising along. Maybe all the strange mishaps we had been experiencing were finally over. That is until about mid-morning, when I looked up ahead, and all I could see was white. White fog just rolling along on top of the water. I knew we would soon be swallowed up in it. Knowing how dangerous it was to continue on in the fog, I was tempted just to throttle back and hang out until it lifted. This was one time when we desperately needed that chart plotter. If we had one, we could have just motored along without running into shore.

But here we were, far from the shore and I didn't like the idea of just sitting dead in the water for someone to run into. I looked around trying to get my bearings before it went completely white. I could see no land anywhere. I took a guess and turned sharply to the West, where I knew the shoreline was. I slowed down to half speed and grabbed the fog horn.

I blasted it every once in a while because I didn't know what else to do. Twenty minutes went by and we were just swimming in fog. We couldn't even see the bow of our own boat. It was totally white and utterly quiet, other than the slow rumble of our idling diesel motor down below. I turned even a little more for land. Both Lilly and I stretching our necks for any hint of where we were. Then out of nowhere... came the clearest voice of a small child, "Will you pass me a hotdog please?"

I jammed the throttle off, and shifted full astern. For a few seconds the fog parted. There—dead ahead— not twenty feet in front of us was a picnic table with a family of five enjoying their barbecue. We were so close we were all embarrassed and they politely looked the other way. I tried to act normal as they disappeared back into the fog, and we dropped anchor immediately and stayed put. I had overcorrected and we had drifted into Nanoose

Harbor until we were headed directly onto the finger of land there that sticks out to the water.

In less than an hour the fog had disappeared and we could see where we were going, again. We got back to our compass setting and in a few hours caught sight of a lighthouse in the distance to the East. Still following the coastline on the west side, to a place called Deep Bay, which we knew had to be around here somewhere. At that point, we came upon some brightly colored cork floats looking like floats for a net. It went most of the way across the entrance to the bay. We tried to go around to get past but it seemed to go on forever. Finally I just headed straight into the bay, watching to make sure I didn't drag any of the floats with me.

Once inside, I dropped anchor with great relief, and being exhausted from the stress of our morning experiences, I fell into the bunk for a nap. Somewhere in my sleep, I heard the rumbling sound of a huge boat engine and woke up only to discover the sound was real. What in the world? I stuck my head out of the hatch and found myself starring up into the faces of four angry Coast Guard men.

49.45° N   124.71° W
to
48.8° N   123.3° W

8 Man Overboard!

"We thought you were dead!" the man who was talking sounded irate. "Don't you have your radio on? We tried to call you many times! You just went over a dangerous reef! We thought you were dead!"

I was terribly embarrassed and promised to be more careful on my way out. Their disgust of my seamanship was very apparent. Once again, we were paying for being beginners. I had a feeling that we possibly had been part of another of God's miracles, though, helping us over a reef we had no idea we were even crossing. But it was nice to know we had that kind of backup on our adventure of a lifetime.

Our next stop was in Campbell River, a modern town with a great boat yard. If it were affordable we would finally pull the boat out here and paint her bottom. We arrived late in the afternoon and dared not enter the marinas—they were packed like sardines in there. Instead, we kept looking for a spot to anchor and went farther north of town.

Somewhere along the way, the boat had started to vibrate, which I did not like. Was something falling off? Finally after an hour extra running, we found a great spot to spend the night in. An old cannery in a big bay. We had a great night's sleep without worry. No waves breaking or currents running, it was tempting to stay here, but just too far from town. So, back we went the next morning to find something more workable.

The boat seemed to take forever to get the five miles back to Campbell River. Which was confusing. Even though this area was known for its strong currents and tides, something seemed very wrong about it. There were other boats going past us but we were used to chugging along at our own slow pace by that time and didn't think much about it. Besides that, if there was anything wrong we would see it when we hauled the boat out, later on.

We were trying to get to a less populated spot right across from Campbell River, but time kept going by and we were still not making much headway in that direction. Fortunately, we caught sight of a vacant spot near a small ferry landing. One that seemed to be a short transit across the channel between the town and the island. There were even a few fingers for fishing boats to dock nearby. The tide didn't seem to be so strong going in that direction. So, we inched our way over there and dropped anchor as close to the little marina as possible, without being in the way of the ferry.

Actually, it was a very bad spot. It was not protected at all from the strong tidal currents that screamed through there. Discovery Passage currents boiled past twice a day and made the anchoring rough to say the least. The rocking wasn't that bad, but getting into and out of the dingy was tricky. Up till now, we never got off when at anchor because we were just passing through. But here, we needed to go ashore.

We had to get the bottom cleaned and check some things out. The next leg of our journey included a series of "narrows." So anything I could do while we were here to make sure the *Glory B* was in the best shape possible would be to our advanntage. Having her hauled out and working on her in a boatyard was now a necessity.

Since we had to take the short ferry back across to Campbell River to make an appointment for hauling out, we would have to row our dinghy over to the docks. It was not too difficult—a little tricky climbing into that light little boat which was bobbing in the water about four feet lower than the decks of the *Glory B*. But we went carefully, took our time, and made it.

We had a great day in Campbell River. We found the boat yard and scheduled a date to get to work on her. It was a little more expensive than we expected, but affordable. They even had chart plotters. Twice the price of the ones in the States but now—because of the submerged rocks and reefs in this area that were invisible from the surface—it seemed imperative. At any rate, it was a beautiful spot and the prospects of spending the extra time here were pleasant.

The next day, it was time to see if the check from our renters had arrived as planned. We also wanted to make a trip to the local library, located at the head of the ferry landing. The day before, we had entered the dingy carefully. I had a bow line and a stern line to hold onto while Lilly climbed in. Today, I was a little sloppy.

Glory B!

Not realizing how important those lines were, I just held the bow line. This time, when Lilly stepped into the dingy, a large wave hit the side. Since she had nothing to help keep her balance, she fell toward one corner. In moments, the corner dipped under the water and the little boat started to fill up. I leapt forward to help.

In my haste, I kicked her computer bag into the bay.

Something I didn't even notice until I was pulling her out. Then I saw the bag, bobbing on the water, but still within reach and easily recovered. But as I lifted it aboard and saw torrents of water running out, I knew we were in big trouble. Her new Apple computer, cell phone, passport, and forty pages of the manuscript for her next novel, were ruined.

We went back down below and tried to recover. The papers dried out—a little worse for show but usable. On the other hand, all of the electronics were dripping seawater. There would have been more hope if they had toppled into a lake. But a trip to the nearest computer shop later revealed that any contact with seawater—no matter how brief—had an immediate corrosive reaction on the delicate wiring.

Knowing it would take days for Lilly to recover from the incident, I left her on the *Glory B* and went ashore to finish the business at hand. First, was to find a bank and withdraw enough money to pay for repairs. To my surprise, there were no funds waiting for us. Now we were in an even bigger disaster. Without our knowing, a combination of events had come together to form a virtual "perfect storm" that was dangerously close to swamping our entire adventure. Not to mention our dreams.

The next shock came when I called Oklahoma to find out what the problem was. The renters had not only moved out in the middle of the night, but had completely trashed the place. According to a neighbor, the beige walls had been replaced by rainbow colors accented by graffiti, punctuated by holes throughout the entire house. The airtight stove had been moved into the study and all the built in bookshelves and cabinets knocked out to convert it into something else. They had also rifled through and taken things from the cabin in the back pasture where we had stored all of our own belongings.

The neighbor we had hired to manage things in our absence said it was all so horrible we would have to come home immediately because it was too much for her to deal with. She couldn't see how it would ever get into shape to be rented, again. At any rate, it would be way too much work. I tried to relate that we were in the middle of a disaster, ourselves. In Canada—another country, for heaven's sake—and we couldn't just get home in a day, or two.

At that point, I could see only one option open to us. That was to do everything by phone, right where we were. I placed an ad on Craigslist, offering free rent for repairs in order to get things rolling, again. But it entailed dozens of phone calls to make viewing appointments (another neighbor helped with that) and weed through the applicants to find the best fit for the job at hand. Within a week it was settled.

It would be a tight squeeze for us to wait a whole month without the added rental income. But if we watched our pennies, did most of the boat repair work ourselves instead of taking it into the yard, I figured we could manage it. To top things off, we received a six hundred dollar bill for all that negotiating by phone while traveling through a foreign country, and our phone service was promptly cut off.

Which was another unpleasant surprise

considering we had made arrangements for special rates while traveling through Canada. After a bit of research it was discovered that the agent neglected to activate the program for us. In the end, there was nothing we could do about it.

Our trip of a lifetime was turning into a nightmare right in front of our eyes. I might have been tempted to quit if we weren't already stopped dead in our tracks. The way I looked at it, there was only one thing left I could do.

"Lord, you said you can have whatever you can believe for. So, we've been acting on that. To go to Seattle and get the boat of our dreams was a miracle. To get a roofing job at the age of seventy when one hundred and forty-nine younger applicants had applied was also a miracle. To navigate over a reef that the coast guard said was impossible to cross without piling up was another miracle, too. After all that, I believe in miracles. Now, here we are with all these other things coming at us at once—and I can't see any way out of this situation. But if you're a God who works in miracles...I need one more."

It had been the absolute worst day of the trip and the disasters were far from over. Nothing could be recovered from either the computer or the cellphone.

Glory B!

We spent a few days just trying to get over it all, during which time Lilly began using the old-fashioned pen and paper to write with, and I tinkered around with deck chores. I tried to see how far down I could scrub the boat bottom by pulling myself alongside in the dinghy and using a long-handled scrub brush. It was slack tide—in between tides when the water is perfectly still for nearly an hour—on a beautiful sunny day, and I decided to take advantage of it. As I worked my way aft, I looked down into the clear water at the propeller. It didn't look quite right. By turning the shaft, I discovered there was only one blade left out of three.

Are you kidding me?

According to the laws of push and shove, the boat shouldn't have been able to move at all in that condition. It would cost about six hundred dollars for a new propeller and take a long time for that much money to trickle in. With so much time on my hands, I decided to call around some local places to see if I could find a used one. I discovered there was a repair yard close by, and the owner said he had a good collection of propellers I could look through. To my pleasant surprise, one had the correct shaft size and approximately the right diameter for the *Glory B.*

And the price? Only fifty dollars.

Within a week, we connected with new renters and solved the propeller problem. But how were we going to get it on without hauling the boat out? We had hired a diver to take it off the shaft, but now we couldn't move the boat anywhere, at all. About the time I was thinking we could be stuck here for months, I made friends with a local man who had been working on his own boat, nearby, and watching as I made all my trips back and forth from the docks.

He said he knew of a place that had a grid we could tie up to for free, where we could do all the work ourselves between tides. I had never heard of such a thing. But it seemed in this land of twenty foot tides, it was possible to be "high and dry" for about ten hours at a time between changes. Where was this place? Just around the end of the island, in an abandoned town, on some local Indian Reserve, he said. He happened to be going to that area to do some logging in a few days, and he would be glad to tow us out there. Which seemed like such an answer to prayer, I readily agreed.

What I didn't know then was that the end of this island hung down into the turbulent waters of where the Strait of Georgia and Discovery Channel met, and the abandoned town was on a different island entirely—over thirty miles away. So, when the day came, I took the invitation to ride comfortably with my new friend on top of his fancy sport-fishing boat at speeds much faster than my own boat could achieve even in top condition.

Otherwise, I never would have left Lilly on the *Glory B* alone for that wild ride.

50.19° N   125.09° W

9 Night in a Ghost Town

It was five hours to the grid, during which time I only glanced back a few times to see how the *Glory B* was riding. Dave Taylor, had taken the extra precaution of putting a line on each cleat of the stern of his boat so she would tow more easily. It didn't take long to realize how skilled he was in handling all things boat related. Especially the strong currents so characteristic of this little group of islands known as the Discovery Islands.

It was a stunningly beautiful trip. Once past the choppy point of Quadra Island that took about two hours —during which time I hardly felt more than an occasional jolt—we turned north into Hoskyn Channel, and chugged along for another three. This far north the days were long, with light that stretched until after ten o'clock at night.

After the unexpectedly long passage, I was looking forward to one of Lilly's delicious dinners that we could share with our new friend. I even thought I could smell roast beef by the time we tied up to the grid. At this hour of day, it looked more like two telephone poles sticking out of the water next to the dock. The only difference was that we had to make a complete loop around each one with the dock lines, so that the boat would rise and fall with the water level. At low tide, she would be sitting on her own bottom, high and dry.

We wouldn't be able to do any work until tomorrow but we were more than ready for a good meal and relaxing evening. Except there was no meal waiting for us. For Lilly, the trip around the end of the island had been too rough to cook anything on the stovetop, and she hadn't got her pot roast on in time for it to simmer until tender. Somewhere between eight and nine o'clock she served something leathery to us which our guest was gracious enough to say, "It had a fine good flavor, though," before we all retired for the night. He to his larger, more comfortable accommodations, and ourselves to our much smaller space that looked like a disaster after Lilly's attempts to produce a three-course dinner in that little galley. Up until then, we had been living off soups, stews, oatmeal, and tuna.

Our own bed was comfortable, though, and we felt much better in the morning when we woke up to a brilliantly beautiful day. Absolutely perfect for the kind of work we needed to do. It was a delightful little waterfront town of light blue buildings with white trim, nestled into dense forest. It had two long docks for tying up to, and even a self-service library at the end of one, that was run on the honor system. There were also bicycles there that anyone could ride, if they took a notion to sightsee along the road that was further in. There were several houses nearby with neat wooden fences around the yards, and Lilly couldn't quit talking about how delightful it would be to live in a place like this.

Except there was nobody in it.

The whole place was deserted. It had turned into a ghost town when the cost of fuel dock insurance grew too high for small operations, making it too expensive to keep open even during the busy boating season when so many tourists passed by. Without services, no one had stopped there for years.

Especially with so many other choice towns that offered amenities nearby. Sometime during the late morning, we discovered there happened to be one resident left. He was an older man who had appointed himself a sort of caretaker of the place, who meandered down to see what we were working on.

We didn't have to wait until the tide was completely gone before the propeller shaft came into view, and Dave and I waded knee-deep in the water to start working. We tried to put the new propeller on... no go. The taper was different and it was too small. At that point Dave said we would have to have a new propeller flown in. I had no idea what a float plane cost but I knew I didn't have it. As I saw it, my only option was to somehow make this one work. It was made of solid brass, so was a soft metal. If I had the proper tool I could file it down myself.

I did have a small file but the tide would be back before I could ever get the hole big enough. But I started filing anyway. With nothing left to do, Dave took one of the bikes and went for a sightseeing trip. About a half hour later pleasant things started to happen. A fellow boater, who had been anchored across the channel nearer to Quadra Island, saw us on the grid. He was several miles away but came over in his dinghy to see what was up. When he found out we needed a file, he went all the way back to his boat and got one. It happened to be exactly what I needed.

The hole was big enough to give it another try by the time Dave got back. Close but not quite. After a little more filing he pounded it onto the shaft with a large sledge hammer enough to give it a couple of turns on the threads to keep it there. And that was good. It was then that I realized we still had enough time before the tide came back to put the bottom paint on, as well. Even with all the difficulties, we got everything done we needed to do.

Once again, I wrote it into my log as another miracle. One minute things looked impossible, and the next thing we knew, it was done. How does one explain those things? During our seven hundred and fifty mile trip up the Inside Passage, at the height of the season, there were many other boats going and coming along the same route. There was never a day when we didn't see any pass by. Not only tourists, but ferries, tugboats hauling barges, and even cruise ships went by. No one had ever come to "see what we were doing" before. Especially someone who

Glory B!

happened to have the exact tool I so desperately needed to fix my problem at that moment.

Even though we had encountered many problems along the way, I was beginning to realize that if I asked for the Lord's help, then just made one step, one little step, and then another, God would orchestrate the rest. Whatever the explanation for these two helpful men being there for us at the right time and place, the facts were that the *Glory B* came limping into Campbell River needing serious repairs that would normally cost thousands of dollars to fix. She left with a fast new (to us) propeller at a cost of fifty dollars.

Dave Taylor wouldn't even take any money for gas.

Instead, he said he had enjoyed spending time with Americans on their Independence Day. Was it that time, already? With all that had been going on we hadn't even realized. Being in Canada where there had been no usual decorations to give us a hint, we would have missed it. But once, again, we were taking off under our own power, and feeling the wonderful freedom of it on that special day.

Can you imagine our elation at being on the water under our own power, again! After the bottom had been scraped of barnacles and sea growth, then painted, we had put the *Glory B* in gear only to find that she seemed to literally leap out of the water.

Was it some illusion because we had been sitting so long at anchor or were we really going that fast? After three hours, we started to seriously look for our turn to go north, again, into the Discovery Passage and back to Campbell River. The trouble was, while we thought we were following the exact route we had taken with Dave Taylor, we could see no place to turn in.

Where had the opening gone?

Up until now, our average speed had been five to six knots per hour. Later we would discover that we had been flying along at least eight, and the throttle wasn't even pushed all the way forward. However, the boat wouldn't go any faster past that point, but instead began to blow black smoke. Not wanting to overload the engine, I kept it backed off. But it was a great pleasure to still feel her shooting through the water even at the reduced RPMs.

It wasn't until later that we found our pleasure was also our mistake. We were still having trouble knowing where we were. We had an emergency tracking device on the *DeLorme*, but the dot that showed where we were was about twenty minutes behind real time, and I got confused. The coast line to the west kept dipping farther south. I took a closer look at the chart and realized we were now closer to the town of Comax to the south than Campbell River to the north. Somehow, we had ended up thirty-five miles farther south than we intended to go right back into the Strait of Georgia.

While it was irritating to have to backtrack to return to our course, it had been a long day and we decided to anchor in Comax Bay for the night rather than continue on. Especially since the wind and waves were picking up here in the Strait of Georgia that stretched all two hundred and eighty-five miles along the east coast of Vancouver Island.

A plan we thought reasonable all the way up until we ran out of gas.

49.67° N   124.92° W

10 A Series of Divine Appointments

For the second time on our adventure we found ourselves dead in the water. However, for the first time on our adventure, we not only had enough wind to sail, it happened to be blowing in the right direction. I lifted the sails and in no time she reached the same fast clip she had been making under power. Never had she sailed so beautifully and we were caught off-guard by the feeling of elation it gave us.

We were also at such a perfect angle that there was no need to tack until the very last minute when we turned into the anchorage in front of the marina. I dropped the sails and we ghosted along in total silence. When we came into a fairly wide spot between two other boats, I let go the anchor and listened to the chain rattle out until it hit bottom.

Glory B!

These were the kind of moments I had been dreaming about. There would be plenty of time for rowing over to the gas dock, tomorrow, and taking care of some of the temporary fixes I had been making along the way. Right now, I just wanted to sit back and enjoy the beauty of the place.

We were awakened the next morning by a couple of young voices right next to our boat.

"Are you going to scream like a girl, again, when we dump, today?"

A much younger voice replied, "I'll try not to."

I stuck my head up out of the hatch and discovered we were right in the middle of some sort of junior sailing regatta that was about to commence. There were dozens of identical little sabots bobbing about, along with three motorized skiffs racing back and forth, with older teens hollering out instructions. It was a sight I would never forget and something stirred within me.

Having done some sailing with kids in earlier years, myself, I discovered that most parents were not willing to let their children go out onto the ocean in the sort of small craft that almost always tipped over at some time during the day. While we had resigned ourselves to taking our own children and occasionally a few of their friends on such adventures, here was a group of people that seemed to have worked out all the problems for larger activities, right in front of our eyes.

Not only were the little boats so buoyant they wouldn't sink even when upside down—but the skiffs were strategically placed so that the minute one did tip over, the nearest skiff raced to fish the floating occupants out via a boat hook. They then hurried them back to shore to get out of their wet clothes and watch the rest of the race. The point of which was to make it all the way around a certain buoy in the bay and back without capsizing. That day, there were only two out of the dozens who didn't tip their boat over.

We later discovered that this was some sort of week-long day camp that started early enough to catch the calmer waters of the morning, and be finished after lunch each day before the real wind and chop turned the bay too rough for any but the stoutest of boats. Our own tender dinghy was not safe in these waters in much of anything over five knots of wind.

As the week went on, I began to notice the smaller details of success. Such as a mixing of the ages: there was always an older child paired with a younger one in each boat. Which surprisingly brought the best out of everyone involved. The younger ones had great respect for the older ones, who in turn were very patient with their instructions and never bullied or spoke harshly to them. The results were the pride and thrill of learning to sail, as well as the underlying bonus of giving and garnering respect for each other. All of which made our unexpected side trip to Comox one of the high points of our entire trip.

The next day we paddled into the marina where I purchased five gallons of diesel fuel and went through the steps of purging the air out of the fuel lines. I had learned back in Fisherman Bay, when I had the engine torn down, that all the air had to be bled out before turning it on, again. Now, having run it all the way out of gas, I would have to do the same thing. Fortunately I had done this several times, already, so I had the engine running again in no time.

On my way back and forth to the docks I noticed there were two grids at the end of the marina. Easily recognized now that I knew what they were for. So, I stopped into the office and found we could get on for very little money. I would finally be able to replace the rubber strut bearing that was old with a new one. I wanted to break out of this disaster mode, so decided to do all I could to keep the boat going before it broke down instead of after. The only thing was, we would have to wait a couple of days and pull it over at midnight in order to catch a high enough tide to get onto it. But we didn't mind.

Comox was a beautiful town with the perfect bay and it would be a pleasure to explore more of it.

Now that we were familiar with the simplicity of getting on and off the grid we had no problems other than having to do so in uncomfortably tight quarters in the pitch dark. However, there was absolutely no other boat traffic to contend with at that hour, so things were working in our favor. By the next morning, the tide had gone out and we were able to perform the simple task of replacing the strut bearing and we were off, again, with the next high tide.

As we were weighing the anchor and getting ready to leave the town of Comox, we were hailed by a young couple in a small sloop who wanted a tow. After sailing up from Seattle, they couldn't get their engine started and had run out of vacation time. They decided to find someone who was leaving and could pull them out into the Strait of Georgia, so that they could pick up enough of the steady southerly winds that were so prominent this time of year, to simply sail home.

Which we were more than happy to do. We tied them about twenty feet off our stern and were soon chugging out of Comax Bay and into the long channel. It was a beautiful morning, and as I sat wondering if the winds would hold up all the way back for them, I suddenly had a thought.

"Do you have a diesel engine?" I called back to the young man, who was sitting on his bow as we went along. "One of the first things to try is bleeding the fuel lines of any trapped air." For once, I knew what I was talking about since I had just finished doing the same thing, myself.

He hadn't thought of that. So, he jumped down below and tried his luck at bleeding the lines. Within fifteen minutes, we heard the sound of his diesel engine starting up and then an excited shout. A few seconds later he popped up out of the hatch and was up on the bow, again, with a big smile.

"It worked!" He pointed emphatically at me. "You are the man! Thank you!"

I realized then that—almost imperceptibly—I

was becoming much more adept at things which had caused us so much anxiety at the beginning of our trip. Things like setting the anchor or pulling up to a crowded gas dock began to become commonplace after so much practice. And after having been on the receiving end of help from other knowledgable sailors, it felt wonderful to be able to share a bit of the same with someone else.

When we finally said goodbye to them and turned our separate ways, I had never felt so good about the shape the *Glory B* was in. We had done everything we could at this point, she was running beautifully, and the weather forecast told us we should be able to make it all the way to Seymour Narrows, that same day. Once again, we would be entering an entirely different environment than we had ever experienced. A succession of "narrows" and "straits" that would stretch all the way up through Canada, commonly known as the Inside Passage to Alaska.

We felt almost as elated as when we had left Liberty Bay. Since then, we had been through many mishaps and difficulties but—true to His promises—the Lord had brought us through even the unexpected ones. Now, we were more than ready to continue our "adventure of a lifetime" safely tucked away from the giant, often turbulent, waters of the Pacific Ocean in these uniquely protected areas.

Or so we thought.

from the

Photo Album…

LOG OF THE GLORY B.

Pender Island to Campbell River
128 Nautical Miles

On a beach at the tip of San Juan Island. Behind us is Canada... somewhere.

Rowing back to the Glory B on beautiful Fisherman's Bay... Rowing back in the fog...

Setting sails for the big adventure.

"The trip seemed to be one obstacle after another so far... but they only looked impossible."

Sailing into Nanaimo, our first city in Canada.

A Haven in the Wilderness...

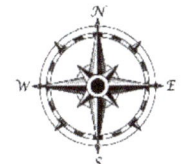

Rocks! Now I know what that marker means...

Lilly holding on for a fast ride.

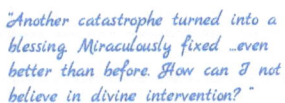

"Another catastrophe turned into a blessing. Miraculously fixed ...even better than before. How can I not believe in divine intervention?"

LOG OF THE GLORY B.
Campbell River to Port Hardy
2014

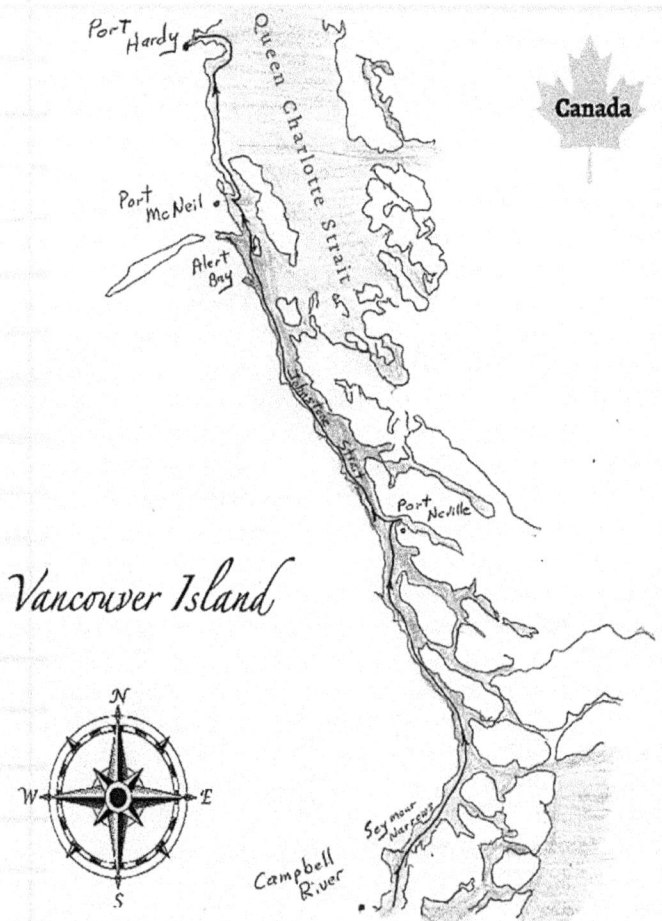

Part Three

Comox to Port Hardy

50.14° N   125.35° W

11 Narrow Places

We had heard a lot of fearful talk about the difficulties of going through the narrows. Ten miles ahead, where the narrows began, is where the strong currents started. These pinched areas of the Inside Passage—Seymour Narrows, the Johnstone Straits—all the narrow areas where when the tide is moving up to fifteen knots and your boat is only capable of four or five, you have a problem. The real problem was that neither Lilly nor I had ever been in these kind of waters and we didn't know what to expect. We were looking for adventure but within limits. We would like to still have our boat at the end of the trip, and we didn't want to get wet.

Our first big challenge—the Seymour Narrows—lay ahead. The larger area north of them, another

Glory B!

channel known as Johnstone Strait, was being pushed by an even bigger body of water called the Queen Charlotte Strait. Each time the tide switched from flowing north to south, it barreled through the smaller Seymour Narrows at eighteen knots. Much faster than the *Glory B* could ever go on her own. A situation that carried the real danger of being pushed backwards onto the rocks. Something I had spent hours worrying over before we even got there.

Less than a mile long, it had been known as the most dangerous stretch of water on the Inside Passage for a hundred years: the cause of over a hundred shipwrecks between eighteen fifty and nineteen fifty-three, with the loss of many lives. Captain George Vancouver described it as "One of the vilest stretches of water in the world."

That's because there were two mountain peaks just below the surface of the narrow channel which created a "perfect storm" situation. The forceful current and swirling waters around them would cause ships to be torn up on the jagged peaks, then immediately sucked back out into deeper water where they would quickly sink. The infamous spot came to be known as Ripple Rock even though it wasn't really a rock, at all.

Because of the tremendous force of the currents there were no simple solutions. The first attempts were to anchor a huge barge on one of the submerged summits long enough to drill holes so it could be blasted apart. The steel cables would not hold the barge and broke many times before any holes could be drilled deep enough. Finally, a team of scientists from *Canada's National Research Council* came up with a plan to tunnel into them from nearby Maud Island to avoid the strong tidal currents on the surface and come up from underneath.

After twenty-seven months of drilling, and thirteen hundred and seventy-five pounds of Nitamex 2H explosive, a network of tunnels packed with the explosive hurled three-hundred and seventy-thousand tons of rock into the air, creating the largest non-nuclear explosion ever to occur on the planet.

We heard this story personally, from an expressive store clerk in the little town of Quathiaski, on Quadra Island, who described the event with great excitement and detail, as if it had happened only the week before. When we finally made the passage, ourselves, fifty-six years later, the reputation of Seymour Narrows still lingered even though the dangers were much subdued. We drifted through the seemingly inconsequential area peacefully, with only a few slight whirlpools that looked much the same as many other places we had traveled through. With the added confidence of our clean hull, fresh coat of bottom paint, and a more powerful propeller to move us along, we were able to enjoy ourselves more than worry about things for the first time in many months.

That day, we hit it just right and shot smoothly through the narrows on the north-rolling tide. We dropped anchor just a mile north in a place called Deep Bay. Our first day of resuming our adventure had been a success. There was a lot of daylight left but I was taking no chances. Any more disasters and I'd be on this trip by myself. I naturally love the wild outdoors and this place was beyond my expectations. There seemed to be wildlife everywhere. What a pleasure to share our next morning with little families of ducks bobbing around or gliding close to the boat, as if we were as much a part of their landscape as they seemed to us.

Up on deck, the next morning, as I was preparing to get underway, it seemed quite windy in this protected little spot behind a tiny island I had nudged the *Glory B* up against. Something made possible because there was often more than a hundred feet of depth so close to the land one could tie a line onto a tree and still not touch bottom in this area. I turned the VHF weather channel on only to discover the forecast was predicting forty knot winds out of the north, and waves with a three to four foot chop. Way beyond Lilly's comfort zone. Considering she was still game after so many disasters, I decided to play it safe and hang out another day in this beautiful little cove.

When we finally got underway, again, and pushed out into the Johnstone Strait—that place on the map we had been aiming at for so long—we settled into a routine that was to become our "new normal" for the next couple of weeks. We would begin our travels with a second cup of coffee at the helm, continuing our course heading as spectacular views of heavily wooded islands rose up on both sides like an unfolding ribbon all day long. But we were not all by ourselves out there.

Our compass setting for the day was three hundred degrees. Something that was becoming more important to me as time went on. When we first began our trip, I thought I could stick close to the

Glory B!

shoreline and check what I saw against the maps. But I was quickly discovering that did not work. Moving around points of land—or rocks—bumped us off course too easily. Getting farther into the channel took care of that, and allowed us to keep our course heading for longer periods, and sometimes all day long.

We no longer had to worry about getting lost because we were in a narrow channel. We could see both sides—which were often less than a mile apart —and all we had to do was follow it along for the next sixty miles. This route was truly a marine highway with tugboats towing barges, occasional cruise ships and fishing vessels passing by on their way to, or from, the larger towns and cities. We dropped the hook that night in a place called Port Neville, where—once, again—we were hit by heavy winds. But that was the beauty of the Inside Passage: a hundred places to pull over when weather gets bad and you have had enough.

Within minutes we were nosing up a little side channel, looking for a protected spot to anchor in. I took advantage of the quiet hours each evening looking over my maps to see what lay ahead of us. At this point I decided I had spent way too much time reading the *Waggoner Cruising Guide*. I had been following those detailed descriptions more than the maps, only to discover there were many times they seemed to stretch the danger factor beyond what our actual experience of the place was. Which could have been an "ignorance is bliss" situation on my part.

Anyway, we passed through the entire area unscathed and enjoyed all of it. Especially our occasional glimpses of migrating whales, hundreds of sea lions, and dolphin escorts that would dart under our boat and have to slow down in order to travel alongside us for a while. With a landscape dotted by Canada's white lighthouses, it was all an incredible feast for the eyes.

For the first time on our journey, I felt like I finally had things under control. I was headed for Port Hardy, the last city on the tip of Vancouver Island--the jumping off place before the long crossing of Queen Charlotte Sound. After that, we would be entering the true wilderness places of the Inside Passage, where the distances were dotted only by small towns and Native villages, threading through hundreds of islands with great swaths of still untouched rainforest on top of them.

Glory B!

At Port Hardy I planned to get detailed charts of the area so that my plotting of our course each day could be more accurate. Up until now, I had been moving along from town to town, even though we often dropped anchor for the night in some peaceful cove before we actually got there. I knew where I was by how many hours we had been traveling on a specific compass heading every day.

After Port Hardy, there would be days between towns for us, at times. Especially when the fastest I could go (without wind or more horsepower) was my usual five miles an hour. I had enough hours at the helm already to know how these islands could start to look identical or familiar if I lost track of where we were.

Up until now, we had been pushed along mostly by unexpected circumstances which dictated what we had to do in order to continue on. From now on, things would be different. By the time we got to Port Hardy, our funds would be replenished so I could buy the charts, and replace the faulty pump that was doing its job so inadequately. I did not want to face that long stretch of open water, which held the notoriously rough Cape Caution at the end, without being as prepared as we could be.

What I wasn't prepared for was what had happened to Port Hardy since the latest *Wagoner's Guide* had declared it "one of the premier destinations for underwater explorers and adventurers of all types" and the way it was, now. Staring at my tourist map I could see it tucked in at the back of Hardy Bay (that was miles long), and seemed almost protected by a string of islands near the front that stretched all the way out into the mighty Pacific Ocean. I was especially intrigued by a place on one of them marked, "God's Pocket."

Surely a place someone had deemed one of the most protected places on earth. Having been rescued so many times on my own journey by forces greater than myself, it was something I could definitely relate to. Something that made me contemplate how wonderful it would be to live in a state of being in "God's Pocket" wherever they went: already covered, protected, and provided for in every circumstance.

A thought that ended up being miles away from what the local name really implied.

50.71° N   127.46° W

12   The Hardest Thing

Toward the end of Johnstone Strait, we had our eyes open for a place called Alert Bay. The owner of Lilly's literary agency had been with the forestry service there in his younger days, and was excited about us passing by the place he remembered so fondly. As with many of the landmarks we followed, it seemed much the same as the dozens of other small towns we had seen.

The waterfront was crowded with fishing boats and it looked like a long trek before we would get past the industrial area to explore the more lively center of the town. Since it was still early in the day for us—and because we had so many delays and setbacks since we started our adventure—we opted to keep going and put a few more miles under our keel. We were eager to get to Port Hardy.

Looking back, I later regretted that we had been in such a hurry through that beautiful area. Just forty miles west, across the island from Alert Bay, was a place that contained the Barrier Islands, made famous by the book *Between Pacific Tides* by marine biologist, Ed Ricketts back in the forties. A pioneering study of intertidal ecology that I had been captivated by, after reading the account of that exploring expedition with his friend John Steinbeck. Those unique waters at the edge of the northern Pacific Ocean are literally teaming with all manner of marine life, which I would have loved to explore, myself.

However, it was also one of the wildest, rockiest, most dangerous spots on the island, and there were many shipwrecks scattered along that coast to prove it. One more reason why I had chosen the safer, Inside Passage to Alaska. The next time we pass that close, I would like to rent a car and do some exploring of my own for a few days.

It wasn't until we came out from the protection of Malcolm Island, that we had our first exposure to the Queen Charlotte Strait. That large body of water was huge compared to the smaller, narrower straits we had been passing through up until then. Immediately, we sensed a change in the water. Instead of the strong currents that had been pushing us along, this area held some of the surging waters of the Pacific that we were passing by.

Which wouldn't have been so bad except for the winds that came up like clockwork every afternoon and roared southward, causing confused seas. These two to three foot choppy waves were the worst for our kind of traveling, since if you headed into one set, you were simultaneously hit on the beam with another set coming from somewhere else. While our seaworthy ketch was in little danger of toppling over, it made for constant rocking and pitching, shaking the daylights out of all things below.

A situation Lilly was definitely not happy about.

So, even though we could have made Port Hardy by nightfall, I opted to roost in a windy, rocky cove with a large family of ducks, rather than tackle Hardy Bay, which was wide and open to Queen Charlotte Strait. It would take almost an hour to cross before we could get to the town. It was a night of constant movement. But our anchor was set and we slept well. Only to find that the situation had changed very little by the time we woke up the next morning.

Like it, or not, we were going to have to endure the discomforts of about two hours of choppy seas in order to get to our destination. The next part of our voyage would be our longest day, yet—ten hours across the Queen Charlotte Strait—before we could finally duck into the shelter of Safety Cove, closer to the mainland side of Canada. Before that, I intended to do everything I could to make sure the *Glory B* was ready for that challenge.

We passed by the far side of the island that held the *God's Pocket Marine Provincial Park*, I had been intrigued with and made a mental note to look for it when we passed by on the other side, when we left. Looking might be all we could do because the lodge there catered to divers wanting to explore what was considered to be one of the best diving spots on the Pacific. Later, we found out the reason it had such fabulous diving opportunities was because of the myriad of rocks surrounding it. Divers came from all over the world to enjoy it.

It was something of an off-year for them that summer, though. Enthusiasm was waning after two fatal diving accidents in the area, along with a fading economy. By the time we dropped anchor as close to the waterfront part of town as possible, we discovered numerous closed businesses, along with a sparse population which seemed mostly made up of children and older people. Most of the others had left to work elsewhere. Information we heard at a local hamburger shop, by an owner who described it as a dying city. Which may not be true, today, since places have a way of going up and down with the times. At any rate, it was not the bustling city we were expecting.

While Lilly went straight to the library to use the Internet for sending back some articles, I headed for the local hardware store to look for the items we needed for the next leg of our journey. What a surprise to find things more expensive than all previous places we had been. Even the cost of paper charts that we had been buying along the way, were outrageous. We would either need to wait for another payday, or go on without.

Later, as we stood on the dock, looking at the *Glory B* a hundred yards away and seeing the violent chopping of the bay, we realized that the afternoon winds had come up while we were busy running our errands. Considering one could drown a few feet from the docks if we toppled over, the ride back was uncomfortably scary. From then on, if we wanted to go to town, we left early enough to get back well before noon. Some days, we didn't leave the boat at all because it was too choppy even in the morning. In short, it was a miserable place for us to be anchored in. So, I decided to leave as soon as the weather settled down enough to get out of there.

On the possibility that it might be more protected at the fisherman's harbor farther along the bay, we walked over one morning to check it out. Only to discover a sign at the head of the docks which read: "If you are waiting for better weather, it's not coming."

What kind of a place was this? While having coffee in a shop nearby that overlooked the harbor, we saw a group of young people dressed in shorts, unloading kayaks and supplies from several vans as if they were merrily headed off to some kind of summer camp. Once, again, we were reminded of Comax, where the locals had acclimated so well to their environment.

It seemed that this entire end of the island which hung out into the place where the great Pacific Ocean and Queen Charlotte Strait clashed into each other, had this kind of wave action all year long. At the same time, the many little rocky channels and coves made for spectacular kayaking and marine life viewing in various remote spots. Obviously, the group was headed to one of those.

Back at the town harbor, where we were getting ready to row back to the *Glory B*, we saw a notice that had been tacked up announcing an annual boat race around the buoy at the head of the bay for the following week. The object was to make it there and back in a homemade craft that would not fall apart along the way. Remembering how the young contestants had been so swiftly fished out of the water back in Comax, I thought—even if that were so—it would take some hearty souls to even attempt it in these wild waters.

If nothing else, the temperatures were freezing. The cold, clear waters that made such an agreeable environment for all manner of sea life, was not so good on the human body for extended periods of time. It was a doorway to hypothermia, a condition that could be deadly within a short period of time.

But even that fact was proven "stretchable" as we spent several afternoons watching families enjoying a square, floating dock attached to the end of the pier with a large open area in the center that was netted in the middle so that children could swim in it. There were benches along the edge for parents to supervise from and plenty of space to spread out towels and warm up between dips. To our surprise, there was a lot of laughter and enjoyment coming from that "ocean pool," every day.

That night, I turned on the weather channel and looked over my map, again. The sign was right: the week-long forecast was predicting more of the same, and we were now in a spot where it was just as bad to go back as forward. Real close to halfway to our goal of Alaska. Why did there always seem to be a bigger and bigger challenges ahead of us? We had never done a ten hour run without the option of being able to stop anytime in a protected cove if we needed to. Not only would there be none of those during our crossing of the wide open water that lay in front of us, but the leaky shaft seal would require constant monitoring of water levels, and a lot of hand pumping with the manual bilge pump if it got any worse.

By that time, I was getting as tired of all the problems as Lilly, and I wondered if we should even go on. Or was I just getting spooked because of the stress? The bilge situation would have to be contended with whether we went forward, or back. Not for as long, but nearly. At the same time, nobody but myself was pressing us to launch out from Port Hardy and enter the biggest wilderness area on this continent just to fulfill some dream I had in my youth. The end was still hundreds of miles away through who knows what. Why should I even go through with it?

I shared these feelings with Lilly, prepared to call the rest of the trip off if she no longer wanted to go on. To my surprise, she was very conflicted over the idea of turning back. Neither of us felt any hope in going back, especially after all the miracles we had experienced to get this far.

Surely, there must be some reason—something the Lord had for us at the end—that we would miss out on if we quit. Both of us were discouraged over the situation and stewed over it for the rest of the night.

We still had not decided when our son, Jason, called the next day, and said he would like to meet us in Ketchikan when we pulled in. It was like a green light suddenly blinking on in front of us.

We were headed for Ketchikan.

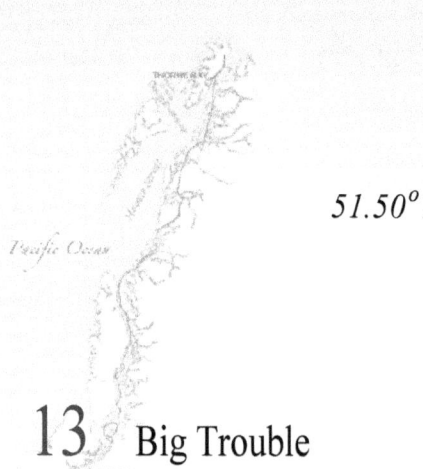

51.50° N   128.50° W

13 Big Trouble

The next day, we woke to the same choppy seas as the day before, and the day before that. So, I decided to just go and get it over with. I had done my homework the night before and knew what the course would be. I laid everything out with a specific amount of time for each compass setting. The first one would be two hundred and eighty degrees along the coast for one and a half hours.

Then we would pass through two giant rocks that would point us right out into the strait. After clearing them, I would turn north and switch to three hundred and thirty degrees. According to my calculations, all I had to do was hold to that heading for the next five and a half hours. That would put us in sight of Cape Caution.

While there is always rougher water around a cape, this one was known for being one of the worst in the area. Another reason why this passage was so stressful. Because of the distance to even get there, we wouldn't be able to avoid the afternoon winds that kicked the seas up even higher at that time every day. But I didn't let myself think about that. Instead, I set my sights on our goal of Calvert Island, five hours beyond Cape Caution. Once there, I would be able to duck into the protection of that piece of land in order to make the final stretch to Safety Cove.

The map for the area we were headed toward was spattered with names like Hurricane Anchorage, Spider Cove, Spitfire Channel, Grief Bay, and Fury Cove. If names were any indicator, we would have to really pay attention and be on the lookout for hazards. Even some of the rocks had names. Once, again, I thought how—in a place where there were rocks along every coastline we passed—those which had ended up on the map must have gotten there by reputation. Whatever the reason, I was going to give them a lot of respect—and a lot of space as we went around them.

Surprisingly, the two giant rocks I was looking

for came into view sooner than I expected. But considering how quickly we had passed up the turn to Campbell River after installing the new propeller, I wasn't going to make the same mistake twice. A fishing boat had been chugging along about a half mile ahead of us but he continued along the coast. Which didn't set off any alarms for me, either. The fishing season was always on for something at this time of the year, and I had noticed how those boats tended to hug the shore where most of the fish hung around.

Another thing that came into play about this time was that the compass occasionally did strange things. That's because the declination varied an entire twenty degrees due to the magnetic pull in these northern areas, as opposed to a mere eight in the more southern waters we were used to. Even though the map I was using was titled *Inside Passage Route Planning Map*, it had a specific note in small print that it was "not to be used for purposes of navigation." Something I had long since disregarded because it was the only detailed one I had after crossing over the border into Canada.

At the beginning of the trip, we had left thinking the marine charts I downloaded onto my iPad would be more than adequate. Especially since that was what almost everyone else was using. The trouble was, they stopped working as soon as we entered Canada. Something about having a limited US subscription without the extended Canadian one. Whatever the reason, they were replaced by something similar to expecting a stick figure to give you a reasonable resemblance to the human body.

Up until now, we had compensated for that by staying close enough to land to pick out the physical characteristics of places we were looking for. A technique made easier by the many detailed descriptions of harbors and their entrances in our *Wagoner's Cruising Guide*. Now, having to cross such a large body of water in a specific amount of time changed all that.

By the time we got out into the strait, the engine had been running for close to two hours. It was time to check the bilge. I turned the helm over to Lilly. Up to that point, we had not been pumping by hand. The spare bilge pump I was using seemed to handle most of it. I still hadn't figured out why it leaked more at some times than others but I definitely wasn't going to let it get ahead of me. So, I decided to use the hand pump and pump it dry every time I came down to look. What I saw shocked me.

I wasn't sure how many gallons it took to fill up the entire bilge but the water was already up to the floorboards. Immediately, I grabbed the big guzzler hand pump, stuck the fat flexible hose out the hatch and over the rail to start pumping. It would take at least fifty pumps to handle all this.

It took a hundred and fifty.

By the time I got the water level down I could feel the strain of all that effort. Doing this every couple of hours, all day long, would be a real chore. I decided to check it, again, in half an hour and went back up on deck to catch my breath. What a blessing that Lilly enjoyed being at the helm. I needed a minute.

It was still early and the water wasn't too choppy. On this compass setting we were headed into the prevailing waves, which was always a smoother ride, and there weren't any cross seas, so far. It would be great if the afternoon winds held off for a while, and I found myself listening more intently to the VHF weather channel chatter.

After half an hour, when I went down to check the bilge, again, I knew we were in trouble. The

Glory B!

water was already in the same spot as before. Without vigorous help from the hand pump this boat could sink! I went to work on it. But by the time I finally heard the welcome sound of the hose sucking air, I knew I couldn't do a hundred and fifty pumps every half hour. Not all day long, I couldn't. I crawled up onto the deck and sprawled out flat on my back to ease the tightness that was already starting in my shoulders.

"Lilly...do you think you could take a turn at the pump, next time? I need a break."

"OK," she agreed quickly. "I can do that."

No sign of panic but only because she didn't realize what a spot we were in. I didn't expect her to do the hundred and fifty. But even if she only did half it would give me the help I needed to catch up with it next time. When her turn came, I took the helm, and she surprised me by doing the entire hundred and fifty before asking if I was ready for lunch. Knowing we were only about two hours away from Cape Caution, where things would get rough even if there wasn't wind, I figured it would be the best time for lunch. My spirits were renewed.

Together, we could do this.

Every once in a while, I would spot a cluster of

rocks uncomfortably close and would have to veer off course a bit to steer around them in case there were others lurking under the surface. They seemed to be all over the place even out here in the middle of the strait. Not long after I got out the map to look over my calculations, again. I spotted a ferry. It was much farther off than they should be. Since we had been following fairly close to the same route throughout our entire trip, one of us was obviously in the wrong place.

I was pretty sure it wasn't the ferry.

About the same time, a new voice broke in to the regular weather channel over the VHF. It was a Coast Guard alert for all boats in the area to be on the lookout for a small sailboat that had left that morning and not yet shown up or checked in at their destination. Several times throughout the rest of the afternoon, we spotted a search plane criss-crossing over the top of us but we never saw another boat in the circle of our horizon. As far as we could see, we seemed to be the only one out there: another reminder of the dangerous area we were traveling across.

On the other hand, I was also becoming more confident in the strong capabilities of this wonderful ketch the Lord had provided us with for our adventure of a lifetime. Having two masts rather than one had more to offer than esthetics, especially for those of us who no longer wanted to spend so much time wrestling with the larger sails and rigging of a single-masted sloop. The seven tons of weight in the full keel also allowed us more stability in rough seas, and multiplied the safety factor by giving it an ability to right itself even if it rolled completely under when knocked over by a large wave.

Because of all this, the *Glory B* was slower than most boats—she did her best sailing in at least ten to fifteen knots of wind—but I felt the trade-off was worth it. She was steadier underfoot, too, which made Lilly happier. She was a "go anywhere in the world boat." Something I had tucked away pleasantly in the back of my mind should the urge ever come on me to do that. Together with her beautifully laid out cabin below decks which allowed for extra comforts, she was a complete home-away-from home, no matter where we dropped anchor. All of which added to our sense of security even in the present circumstances.

I also reminded myself that modern electronics,

like chart plotters, had only been around for the last fifty years. For the thousands of years before, people had traveled over the oceans of the world with nothing more than a compass and sextant. Along with common sense admonitions to watch out for rocks—and for heaven sake—stay well off a lee shore: that place where the wind had grown strong enough to push a boat onto the land.

As expected, the wind came up just when the weather channel predicted. First a little chop, then white caps, waves at one foot, two—and finally as Cape Caution came into view—three to five feet and cross-seas coming at us off the port quarter. But nothing could change the fact that we were committed, now, and would have to deal with things as best we could. Amid the furious crashing and banging of everything we owned down below, we also continued to pump the bilge dry every half hour.

Crossing the Queen Charlotte Strait was most difficult at the end. It would take everything Lilly and I could manage just to make it all the way around that Cape. By then, we were nearing exhaustion but we could not quit. There were no calm places to anchor, nearby and no safe harbors to duck into.

Glory B!

Both of us were at the very limits of our endurance and we still had five and a half long hours to go.

54.32° N   130.32° W

14 Into the Wilderness

The achievement of rounding the Cape—along with the slight settling down of the waves back to the one-to-two foot height that were normal later in the day—was enough to give us a sense of being "over the hump." Things weren't as bad as they could have been. Lilly even felt perky enough to jump down and boil water for our cup of instant noodles we most often resorted to while under way.

We could see land on the starboard side—the mainland of Canada that we had now come close enough to follow along. But we could not miss that southern tip of Calvert Island off the port side which was our "dead reckoning" checkpoint for Safety Cove. I knew that passing by too far away could cause us to miss it, as we had so blindly flown past

Glory B!

the channel to Campbell River, the first day we tried out the new propeller.

There were several tiny islands to distract us from what we were looking for. Egg Island, Table Island, False Egg Island—all of them lined up with my three hundred and thirty degree setting for the coastline. Chugging along at our five miles an hour it seemed to take forever. Finally, four hours later, when I was sure it was Calvert Island on our port side, I dared to get close enough to look for the welcome protection of Safety Cove.

Surprisingly, as soon we got behind the shelter of that Island the whole world changed. Once beyond a place called Grief Bay at the very tip of Cape Calvert and away from the Queen Charlotte Sound, the water laid down almost instantly. That last hour of our longest most difficult day ended in the beautiful peace and quiet of the Inside Passage.

Within minutes of dropping the anchor, we literally crashed into exhausted sleep below.

Waking in the morning to such calm waters and easy sailing, I was overcome by the beauty of the place. The Fitz Hugh Sound was so pleasant. No dingy to cling to, no rough waters, even the constant need for pumping the bilge had been slightly slowed by yet another layer of masking tape I wrapped around the shaft before we started off, again. In this new world, every mile had a cove we could pull into for safety and I slowly began to unwind.

At the same time, we were now in an area that was wild if ever there was wild. Hundreds of little islands, coves—and we seemed to have them all to ourselves. Soon, we were in a place the map referred to as *Hakai Luxvbalis Conservancy Area*, the largest marine park in British Columbia. It was three hundred and four thousand acres that stretched for twenty miles and included Calvert Island, Hecate Island, Nalau Island, and Hunter Island. Set apart as the pristine wilderness it had always been, it was known for being one of their best canoe and paddling areas.

I might have taken time to drop anchor and enjoy some of these wonders if I hadn't still been in survivor mode and bent on making my way to the first full-service marina I could find to repair some of our ever-pressing problems. By the end of the day we were in a place called Shearwater.

The brand new marine facility was modern and packed with boats. There was even a Coast Guard Station with a helicopter pad close to where we dropped anchor at the end of the little channel we turned into to get there. This particular spot had much history as a float plane base and was separated from the actual town of Bella Bella, across the bay. A place we never got to because of the well-stocked marine supply and small grocery store right there at the marina.

The prices were reasonable, too. We bought the new pump and installed it immediately, with no problems. What a relief! In spite of the busyness of the place there were eagles everywhere, perched in trees close to the water, and even in the little city park with tourists walking around snapping close-up pictures. All of which the huge birds ignored. The salmon were coming in numbers, working their way up to the many little rivers and streams of their origins, just like they had been doing for thousands of years.

Leaving the town gave me an uncomfortable feeling. There was no obvious channel, only trees everywhere—crowding close down to the water—giving an almost jungle-like feeling of being pressed in by forest on every side. But I soon discovered that if I kept to my compass setting of three hundred and thirty degrees, a clear path would continue to magically open up in front of us as we moved along.

I followed the map closely, and recognized where we entered Lama Passage—with Hunter Island to the West and Denny Island to the North East. Through endless miles of trees. At times the wilderness was just a few feet away. Beautiful waterfalls randomly showed up and even though we took lots of pictures, we soon discovered the camera put them farther away and could not capture the depth and drama of those fantastic waterslides.

Finally, we entered a larger channel called Seaforth Channel. It was a couple of miles wide and we could at last see an open pathway ahead of us. Truly a "marine highway" through the wilderness, and for twenty miles, we had to change our heading to two hundred and sixty degrees for the first half of the day, then back to three hundred and thirty, again, to enter the town of Klemtu. The community seemed almost hidden in the trees, as though they really didn't want us looking at them. I was constantly surprised that at the end of the day—after all the weaving through islands—that we always ended up just where I wanted to be. I simply had to trust my compass setting.

Something I had learned the hard way by so often

believing what I saw, rather than what I thought I knew.

So many times, we headed into the unknown by faith, truly having no idea what was ahead. What were we really doing here? Why did I feel such a pull toward these places?

One of the major ingredients was my love of the outdoors. It started a long time ago, when—as a teacher—I had been frustrated by the seeming impossibility of "getting through" to my students. Especially the more troubled ones. About the same time, I began taking some required science courses which included field studies that introduced me to the many wonders of the great outdoors. Something I discovered to be even more appealing to children. Later, my own personal enthusiasm led to the development of specialized behavioral training based on motivational outdoor activities.

For the most part, the animal world is hidden from us in nature. But I found the more kids learned about it—the more they personally experienced it—the more they cared about it. The more they cared, the more they wanted to take care of it. To me, it seemed a wonderful answer to the disconnect we were experiencing as a result of so many changes in our society.

While I spent most of my childhood with the freedom to roam the rural spaces outside town, making forts, or rafts, and exploring to my heart's content, most children of today have little or no contact with nature, at all. They are "under stimulated" by missing out on the greatest stimulant available to mankind: the amazing, restorative—often referred to as spiritual—resource known as the natural world. One that is able to teach us, by experience, many of those things we end up seeking all of our lives. It's a place where many of the "whys" of life can be answered. Simply by looking closer. Like staring into a fire—or watching an ocean—are forces that seem to draw us to them.

I don't know why I was so drawn to wilderness places. I only know that forces bigger than myself seemed to be pulling me toward something I had been subconsciously seeking all my life. And I had the feeling I only had to stay on this course I was on to find it. Which was probably the reason we never went ashore there, only dropped anchor for the night in the bay with nothing more than thoughts of a good night's rest and getting back on our journey in the morning. Looking back on it, however, I now know that it was another one of those places I would love to have explored better.

Just that year, the community of Klemtu had completed a wilderness lodge and named it the Spirit Lodge, referring to the rare white bear that was only found in this particular area. It was even possible, now, to take a boat ride in order to observe the Spirit Bear in its wilderness habitat. Had we gone into town we would have found out about the opportunity. But we didn't.

There was so much here we could have experienced had we only taken the time to slow down and look. Something all my quiet contemplations at the helm led me to think was a pretty good maxim for all of life. But I was on my own course at that point and the thought never even occurred to me. Another good example of how so many years had passed before I had my fill of doing more of the things that were truly on my heart.

At the same time, we were within days of coming to the end of Canada and crossing back over the border into the United States. Into Alaska! That illusive goal we had been trying to reach for over a year. Suddenly, we were on a mission. No longer did we take the time to go ashore anywhere. We had a hundred and thirty-two miles of wilderness dotted with only a few coastal towns along the way that we passed right on by.

Instead, we simply moved along as far as we could, each day, then dropped anchor in whatever unnamed cove seemed inviting to us. According to the map, the last town—which was really a city—before crossing the border was Prince Rupert. We were getting a little low on gas so I decided to get some in a town called Butedale rather than dealing with the long crowded lines of the typical city docks farther on.

It was a beautiful town with multiple waterfalls on the surrounding hillsides. We could see many houses and buildings, so dropped anchor across the bay just after dusk and would wait until morning to go over. We had a quiet, peaceful night in the pleasant surroundings, especially with the sound of a waterfall nearby. We even toyed with the idea of finding a nice cafe to have breakfast in before making our final run to Prince Rupert. What a surprise to discover—when the sun came up—that there was no such place. Not for food, or gas, or any other services. The entire place was another ghost town.

Glory B!

On to the big city.

The channel coming into Prince Rupert was full of commercial buildings and we knew we were back to civilization. It was a busy place at the end of July and everyone seemed to be going through Prince Rupert. Maybe it seemed so busy because we had just spent a week seeing almost no one. We dropped anchor across from the town and had a good night's sleep.

But not before I spent my typical hour or so staring at the maps and trying to visualize what lay ahead for our last and final run before dropping anchor in Alaska. We would spend our first night in a place called Foggy Bay, about forty-five miles away. After that, we could head north on our now familiar three hundred and thirty degrees, on a long straight line to Ketchikan.

Rather than backtracking down the long channel we had come in on, it seemed to me there was a shortcut that would save us miles of having to go south before we could go north. It was something called the Venn Passage. Digby Island—where the airport for Prince Rupert was located—was on the port side, and a town called Metlakatla, on the starboard. As I looked to the northwest out of town,

I couldn't see any passage from here. Nothing but rocks. But according to the map, there was one.

Once, again, if I would have had a chart plotter I could have zoomed into a more detailed picture and known for sure. As it was, I decided to take it slow and use caution. At the worse-case scenario we would only have to turn around and go the longer route. Besides that, there were boats everywhere, so there must be something in that direction—maybe a place only smaller boats could get through.

Prince Rupert is on Kaien Island, connected by bridge to the mainland of Canada and the highway system. Travelers going north to Alaska had to either take the ferry, or fly. By July, the tourist season is in full swing and there were tourists everywhere. When we finally got underway, the following morning, I was looking forward to getting back into quieter, less hectic places, and I did not regret my decision to take the shortcut.

We inched along the narrow, less traveled passage for quite a while, avoiding rocks and keeping a lookout for any just below the surface. Finally, the wider water of the Chatham Sound came into view. From there, one could actually look out onto the famed Dixon Entrance, that was known for it's rough, unpredictable seas. This is because it is connected to the North Pacific Ocean. What Lilly and I referred to as "big water." Suddenly, I could see it: my direct route north.

But it was thick with kelp.

Only a short patch, though. Maybe only a hundred yards across. I didn't like the idea of getting tangled up in seaweed but the open ocean was right there on the other side. I could see it. I could also see that little by little we had drawn away from the few other boats that were traveling nearby, who were hugging more toward the smaller Tugwell Island, on the port side. I would have to turn south just to join them. But I was already so close the excitement got the better of me.

I headed in, anyway.

I had never been in such a thick patch of sea growth before. In fact, I had never even—

All of a sudden, there was a huge crunch from underneath and we came to a sickening halt.

from the

Photo Album…

LOG OF THE GLORY B.

Safety Cove to Thorne Bay
335 Nautical Miles

There are no points of land visible on "big water" to orient oneself to. I only had the compass setting I worked out the night before to steer by.

The "doorway" to the Inside Passage.

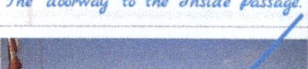

In the narrows, the tide would often roll by 2-3 times faster than we could go. The trick was only to go through when you were going in the same direction.

A trip that held more than we could ever think or imagine...

A night in another ghost town...

Enjoying the journey.

Our favorite cove of all was just a a few miles away from Thorne Bay... but we didn't know that then.

The photo logo Lilly used for all the articles she sent back during our adventure of a lifetime.

Pat "Alaska Gram" Rochester, the first friend we made in Thorne Bay.

LOG OF THE GLORY B.
Safety Cove to Thorne Bay
2014

Canada

Hecate Strait

Part Four

Safety Cove to Thorne Bay

$55.34° N \quad 131.65° W$

15 Crossing Over

We were aground!

Stuck fast on a bunch of barnacled rocks. With visions of a possible crack in the hull, I slammed the engine in reverse, hoping she still had enough water underneath to pull herself off. Thank heaven for that cutaway keel that angled aft a bit instead of going straight down. Slowly, she slid backwards and slipped into the sea. Without a thought to saving any more time, I spun the wheel hard to port and got away from there.

We had skimmed by on a hairsbreadth and only narrowly escaped disaster. The *Glory B* had a much thicker hull than those that had been manufactured more recently, and—once, again—I thanked God for giving me this amazing boat. Lilly did a little yelling at that point and I agreed: no more short cuts for today. This much floating kelp had to be attached to something.

Along with my map studies of the night before, I had also been listening to the weather channel. It looked like it would be a good day. We still had our brush with the Dixon Entrance to face: another large body of water where the sound bumped into the Pacific Ocean without any way to avoid it. But this time—unlike our experience on the Queen Charlotte Sound—there were several spots to duck into if things got too rough.

About midday, we could hide in the lee shore of Dundas Island, in a place called Brundige Inlet. We got there about four hours into the trip. The weather was beautiful, and the seas fairly calm, so we kept going. Two hours beyond Dundas Island was the southern tip of the *Fiords National Monument Wilderness*, where we could duck into a place named simply "Boat Harbor," if we had to. To our surprise, the weather was still holding, so we passed that option up, too.

Going further up into Revillagigedo Channel— and after a full eight hour run—we finally caught sight of Foggy Bay. Although we had known when we were close to the border, it wasn't until we anchored in Foggy Bay, that we could be sure we were finally in Alaska. Being exposed to the rough and tumble of the Dixon Entrance it wasn't as calm and peaceful as the others we had been in. All day, conditions had been perfect for us to cross over.

I went as far back from the entrance as I could, where it would be as calm as possible. There were half a dozen fishing boats already there. Being novices about fishing in Alaska we didn't catch on to the fact that the commercial fishing season had started that very day. Due to the heavy regulations and short intervals, every boat in the industry went out to pull in as many fish as they could. A lot of them with little to no regard for whatever the weather conditions were. Probably the reason it was considered one of the most dangerous jobs on the planet.

We were up early the next morning. After almost two years reaching for our dream, we were excited about being only one day away from our goal. All was good. When we pulled out of the bay and back into the channel—glad to be going north with the protection of many islands along the way between us and the Dixon Entrance—the whole horizon was full of fishing boats.

As far as we could see, they were scurrying all over the place, stretching their huge nets from one end to the other, vying for space like beach-goers trying to squeeze into any spot a towel would fit. At first glance, it looked like I had plenty of room to get through. But just as I started to pass between two large boats, a small high-speed skiff came roaring out to meet us, with an extremely irate man at the helm. I looked at the cork floats of a net, right next to us, trying to decide which way to go to get around it. Was there some rule about passing on a certain side of these things?

He came up to us full blast, waving his hands and shouting, demanding what we were doing in language I wouldn't repeat. We moved off in the direction he waved us and he returned to patrol the edge of his net, making sure no one else came too close to the line. I realized they all seemed to have their own little "guard boat" on duty and tried not to take the incident too personally.

Instead, I did my best to stay out of their way and sent Lilly forward on the bow to look for the little floats that held up the outside edge of the nets, as we slowly weaved our way through. The boats seemed to be going as close to the rocks as they could, so it was nerve racking. I started longing for the first glimpse of the entrance to Ketchikan, where we could drop anchor somewhere and catch our breath. At least there was no need to search for the channel entrance. Before we even got close, we found ourselves joining an ever-growing group of pleasure boaters all headed to the same port.

We were in the channel to Ketchikan.

The little city had a population of less than ten thousand. Still, it was listed as the fifth largest city in Alaska. It sits in a perfect spot for the tourist trade—just over the Canadian border—and is the official gateway to beautiful Southeast Alaska. That area also known as "the panhandle," which is made up of thousands of islands entirely covered over with the largest temperate rainforest in the world: the *Tongass National Forest*. It is the largest forest in the US, covering seventeen million acres that stretch all the way from the Canadian border to spill onto to the mainland of Alaska, about five hundred miles north.

Established by Theodore Roosevelt in 1902, it is dotted by large swaths of wilderness areas that are still wild and unexplored. Rugged mountains and dense forest make them virtually impenetrable for any but the most hearty enthusiasts. While rich in natural resources—including precious metals—the cost of getting them out is more often prohibitive. Meanwhile, the Tongass Rainforest has remained in a constant state of controversy since its very inception.

Industry, ecology, Native land holdings—and the enormity of governing a state that spans a size that equals one-third of the entire United States—all have their own legitimate concerns. Such as stories like the one we heard about the Queen Charlotte Islands where a forester named, Grant Hadwin, was arrested in nineteen ninety-seven for cutting down the "ancestral tree" —the Golden Spruce that was thousands of years old—belonging to the Native tribe in Port Clements. He later realized he could hang for it. Although he disappeared in his canoe somewhere between islands before his court date, the story stuck with me as a reminder that this place I had been trying so hard to get to was not only wild and vast, but very young compared to the rest of the modern world.

At the same time, Alaska has a draw like few other places for being on the "bucket list" for avid tourists. Every year, they flood in by the millions via cruise ships, airplanes, ferries, and private sea craft of all shapes and sizes imaginable. Where the throngs came from so fast, I had no idea. I only know that scuttling up the protective Tongass Narrows to escape the craziness and confusion of day two of the commercial fishing season had somehow turned into a scene that was even worse. And it didn't get any better.

As Ketchikan came into view, I saw multiple Cruise ships, five and six stories high, each containing thousands of tourists, were squeezed alongside docks that were crowded to bursting with boats. Ferries were coming and going from all points north and south, as well as the float plane base where the small private airlines had to land and take off down the center of this same channel we were all trying to crowd into. Some of them were so close as they passed overhead they seemed only a few feet above our masts. After what we had been through, it all seemed like pandemonium.

We scanned the docks for any open slip to pull into just to get out of the way. We knew our first priority was to check in at customs but saw no signs or transient docks where we could do that. In the end, we pulled into the first vacant slip we found, tied up, and I went looking for some place official to report to. I found a small office with several busy people and was surprised at their friendliness. We had definitely changed from "big city culture" and it was most pleasant.

I called customs from the marina office and then returned to the boat to wait for the arrival of the agent who would look us over. My explorations had revealed that—while we had unknowingly chosen a slip that was vacant for at least a few days—the overnight prices were prohibitive for us. Normally, I would have simply gone across from the marina and dropped anchor somewhere. Except the Ketchikan International Airport was directly across from us and because of all the traffic the only place anchoring was allowed was too far out of town for us to go back and forth. It looked like our only choice was to find the next closest community a bit farther off the beaten path.

After a brief walk around town to get our bearings we found a stack of free tourist guides in front of the local mall and sat down at a table to look through one. It was full of spectacular photos and wonderful descriptions of every town in Southeast

Alaska, from Ketchikan to Haines. Our original destination we had been shooting for was Wrangell, but it was still quite a distance away. At our typical five miles an hour, it would at least be an overnight. I decided to call ahead to get more information.

To my surprise, there was no room for us in Wrangell, either. Not unless we went to a private marina about five miles out of town. Without a vehicle and no amenities that far out, I didn't see how that situation would work. Back to the tourist guide. There were a couple of towns fairly close to us across the Clarance Strait, on a huge island called Prince of Wales. Since we had been so focused on the ferry route we had been following, and staying away from the Pacific Ocean side, we hadn't even looked in that direction.

Noticing an attractive ad for Coffman Cove, I decided to call there, first. Especially since the listing included a grocery store, gas station, and a library with Internet. First question: did they have room for a thirty-two foot ketch? Not only did they have room, they were half the price of the slips in Ketchikan. And, yes, there was also plenty of room to anchor out in the bay if we would rather do that. As if that wasn't enough, the conversation ended

Glory B!

with a friendly, "Please come!"

All we had to do to get there was make it through seven hours in the wide open Clarance Strait: which had that unpredictable Dixon Entrance pouring into it from this end. I glanced at the colorful map included in the guide. At the top end it was connected to the even wider Sumner Strait. A huge body of water coming straight off the North Pacific Ocean.

Big water.

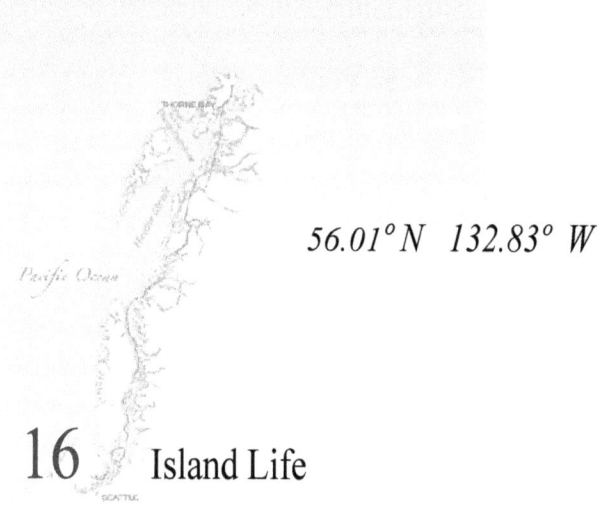

56.01° N   132.83° W

16   Island Life

Early the next morning I headed up to the marina office to pay off our bill. I wanted to get all the way across the Clarence before those predictable afternoon winds came up to stir up the seas. I had taken a closer look at the eastern side of Prince of Wales Island, the night before, and noticed there were many places for us to duck into if things got rough.

Even though the door was open, no one seemed to be on duty inside the Ketchikan office. After walking down several fingers of the crowded docks I finally ran into young woman who looked fairly official, told her I was leaving, and would like to pay. She said she was busy at the moment and suggested

I just send her the money after we got to Coffman Cove.

Had I heard her right? She was so friendly and personable as she waved me off, I realized what a pleasant place we had come to. That she would so willingly trust a perfect stranger made me realize that we had truly broken free of the untrusting disease of big city living and come into a different land altogether. It was huge, wild and remote, with little pockets of people whose very lifestyle made it necessary for them to trust and depend on each other.

From Ketchikan it was two hours of heading north to the Behm Canal, where it emptied into the Clarance Strait. From there, I set the course back onto our familiar setting of three hundred and thirty degrees, picked a far off point of land that I knew to be past the lower third of Prince of Wales Island which hung down into the Pacific Ocean and holds what the maps refer to as wilderness areas.

Little wisps of fog made it feel more illusive and far-off but the sea was calm for us. From here it would take two hours to cross the strait, another two hours to follow the Kasaan Peninsula north before reaching Tolstoi Bay, which seemed like a good place to spend the night before the next day's five hour run to Coffman Cove. We could have made it in one long run, but by that time we were looking forward to some peace and relaxation before heading into anymore unknown situations in unfamiliar areas.

Tolstoi bay was huge, facing more southerly than we expected, and didn't seem to have any place protected to tuck into. Maybe this wasn't Tolstoi Bay. All day we had been passing shallow bays and inlets and I couldn't be exactly sure what I was looking for anymore. Especially using my tourist maps which were known to be more of a representation of places and not true enough to be used for navigation. Just a bit farther up there was a little town called Thorne Bay, tucked quite some distance past a narrow passage one would have to get through to get there. Maybe that would be better.

We passed what looked like a perfect place, called Snug Anchorage, but continued on a bit in search of the town. When we came to the narrow entrance marked by a buoy, it was full of rocks on both sides, and a wall of forested land we would have to skirt around to see any farther. Not knowing how much farther off the town was—or over and behind what—we decided to return to Snug Anchorage.

Glory B!

And snug it was.

We had the peaceful little spot all to ourselves. There were eagles passing by and calling to each other, huge salmon leaping out of the water every few minutes from all directions, and the evening sun so unique to these northern latitudes was warm on the deck. I dropped anchor and we enjoyed one of the best spots of our entire trip. When I finally hauled it up, again, the next morning, we felt gloriously rested and ready to meander back into the Clarence Strait and the last five hours of our long voyage.

The first three hours were sunny and beautiful as we scudded past places like Forss Cove and Ratz Harbor but there were no signs of civilization, just pristine wilderness with streams or rivers pouring in. Most of our travels took us past dense forest that reached all the way down to the tideline along rocky cliffs where the bottom branches were so straight and uniform it looked like some giant hand had come along and trimmed them all into perfect order. And maybe it had. Because the line between trees and sea was precise, with each one staying strictly on its own side. It reminded me of that verse of scripture that describes how God set down the decree that the sea may go this far and no further. And so it has remained.

This trip of a lifetime had turned into something much bigger than we realized. Had we known how hard it would be and the many disastrous situations we would have to face—due to how little we actually knew about taking on such a thing—I'm not so sure I would have even pursued it. Much less been so driven to finish.

Many times over it had taken every ounce of strength and ingenuity I possessed, along with some I had no idea were in reserve. Looking back over the many "divine appointments" and miraculous rescues, I was beginning to know beyond a shadow of doubt, that Lilly and I had not been all on our own out here. Someone bigger than ourselves had not only been with us, but given us draws on reserves much greater than our own. It seemed like an awful lot of trouble to go to, simply for some senior citizen to experience the "trip of a lifetime." Does He really care about me that much?

Or, was there something more?

Things had been so intense I hadn't really put that much thought about what we would do after we got here. Some exploring, surely. Or just saying, "Hello from the *Glory B*," to the friendly communities that

Glory B!

dotted the islands. About the only thing I knew for sure was that neither Lilly nor I was ready to turn around and retrace our steps back home, yet. After what we had just come through, we at least needed some rest to let the stress of the last couple of weeks drain away.

Our first hint that we were in the right place was seeing several houses along the waterfront just before a small island we needed to get around before entering Coffman Cove. By that time it was a little after one in the afternoon and already the wind was stirring up a chop on the water. But—as had happened so many times before—we rode in just ahead of it and headed for the busy little marina that came into view.

The place was more crowded with sport fishing boats rather than commercial craft. But not full to bursting, the way Ketchikan had been, and not even half as big. We pulled into one of the empty slips I had been directed to during my phone conversation. A friendly stranger meandered over to help us tie up, and within minutes, we were hooked up to water and electricity, with all the comforts of the modern world available in our little floating home.

The first thing that caught our attention was a

fish-cleaning station on the docks, not far from where we were, which seemed entirely operated by a single teenager. It was a simple structure, just a covered area held up by wooden posts, with a huge stainless steel table where a girl was cleaning fish so fast it was hard not to just stand and watch her.

It took less than ten minutes for her to cut and fillet a fifty to sixty pound halibut, and only around five for a huge salmon. We later found out that she was paying for college with the summer job and had been doing it for a long time. By eleven in the morning she had already filled many ice boxes for the sport fisherman who began bringing in their catches in a continuous stream all day long. There were a couple of other tables there for people who wanted to do it themselves, but most of the time there was a line waiting to have it done for them.

A little secondary enterprise going on down at the docks was carried out by nine to twelve-year-olds who would "jig for bait" in the morning and evenings in this spot where the constant washing down of the cleaning tables between catches would draw seagulls, crabs, and the smaller fish that were so good for catching the bigger ones. These children would often arrive on four-wheelers with a bucket or two tied to the back, jig for an hour or so, then deftly maneuver backwards along the docks to a place wide enough to turn around before driving up the long ramp to shore, again. No goofing off or playing around: they were working. They also seemed to be extremely happy.

As usual, Lilly wanted to go to the library, first, and get started on some work. Since the loss of her computer and cell phone, we were no longer able to produce the kind of photos and video clips we had been sending back to readers about our experiences along the way. But she had an idea that she could still keep up with her monthly column in a book club magazine by finding local stories, along with photos that others had taken on their own particular adventures of this unique place.

As we crossed the marina parking lot on our way into town, I noticed a teenager pulling out of one of the spaces in a brand new truck. Being an old school teacher who still enjoyed striking up conversations with young people, I called out to him, "Looks like Dad let you borrow the truck, today."

Immediately, he stuck his head out the window with a big smile. "This is my truck," he corrected me. "Paid for with my own money." There was such a happy sense of pride in his voice I couldn't help feeling the pleasure of it with him. Later, we discovered this early maturity and inner resourcefulness to be a common trait to the island youth. Something I appreciated much more having spent most of my career encouraging children to do more—not less—than what they were capable of. Here were many true-life examples of the effects that could have. We did not have to "be on the lookout" for interesting characters as we made our first walk through town that day—they were everywhere.

There was one small building across the street from the waterfront that held what was known in frontier days as a "mercantile:" a single store that sold a little bit of everything. Convenience store items and even a smattering of hardware, fishing tackle, and household goods. Next to that was a hamburger place where orders were taken at the open window and diners ate at the wooden picnic table outside. There were houses on either side—some quite large—that we later discovered to be lodges that catered to all the fisherman that streamed into the area.

The library, post office, and city buildings were

a block farther up the hill. The library had a long covered porch in the front with a row of benches and rocking chairs where patrons could still sit and use the Internet during hours they were closed. Or make a phone call. It turned out that phone service worked best in that specific location and there were always several conversations going on as one went inside. Some were even talking in various corners of the book shelves, too. But the most startling thing about the library was discovering there was a pizza take-out counter in there. Right next to the nonfiction area.

I'm not too much of a pizza fan, myself, but I have to say they also had some of the best homemade pies I had ever tasted, too. We later got to know the couple that ran the little business and ended up attending the same church while we were there. As I walked around checking out the reading material, an outgoing older woman came up and introduced herself to me. She was here for two weeks with a mission team from Seattle, and invited Lilly and I to a community dinner they were hosting that night.

Little did we know how much of a divine appointment that night would be.

Because of the special event, there were more

than just the residents of Coffman Cove in attendance. People had come from all over the island —some from over eighty miles away—to participate in the activity. Considering there were only about three thousand people living on the island, most of them concentrated in the Native communities and one small town on the ocean side of less than about fifteen hundred, there were numerous pastors who had come with numbers of their own congregations, as well. We personally met four of them that evening.

By the time we sat down at a crowded table to enjoy the wonderful selection of food everyone had contributed to—including many variations of fresh-caught salmon and halibut which would have cost a small fortune in any restaurant back home in the "lower forty-eight," we had already introduced ourselves many times. So, when a man seated across the table from us asked where we came from, I answered rather casually that we had sailed here in our boat and arrived just that afternoon.

"Where from?" he asked.

"Seattle," I replied. "Took a lot longer than we expected because we broke down a couple times. And it wasn't as easy without a chart plotter."

Glory B!

He stopped eating and looked at me in utter amazement. "You came across the Dixon Entrance without a chart plotter?"

"I didn't intend to but they were too expensive everywhere we pulled in. I'll get one before we head back, though."

By the end of the evening, I ended up having told the story over and over, and answering questions of our "hows and whys" in more detail, surprised at so much interest in some older couple living out their "trip of a lifetime." Especially in a place where a large portion of tourists were doing the same thing. What was so different about us? That's when I began to sense that something much bigger was going on.

A something I was distracted from over the next couple of weeks as we discovered things in Coffman Cove were not exactly what the visitor guide had advertised. While the marina fees were more than reasonable, the use of electricity was not. It was calculated by the day at a rate that would topple our monthly expenses nearly four hundred dollars beyond the basic slip fee. Considering we had a great battery system that was supplemented by solar energy, we could probably get by with recharging with shore power only a few times during the month.

Except there was something a little more pressing than electricity. The little convenience/hardware store was the only place to get groceries without making a hundred and twelve mile round trip to the larger towns of Craig and Klawock. There was also a "real grocery store" in the smaller community of Thorne Bay that was closer, but one had to take a rough and winding dirt road that amounted to over fifty miles to get there and back.

I considered hitchhiking but one could wait a long time for a car to come by on such long stretches of lonely roads through the forests and mountains of this huge island's wilderness places. So, unless we wanted to live off potato chips, Vienna Sausages, and other snack items for weeks on end, I would either have to try and find a local who was going to one of these places sometime soon, or start looking for another town that was more convenient for people, like us, who had no car.

Once, again, I got out my maps.

Getting to the two largest towns was not an option for us at this time. They were on the "big water" side of the island, facing directly out to the mighty Pacific. To get there, one had to head north out of the Clarence, then make a wide loop around the wild north end of the island via the much larger Sumner Strait, then weave through countless little islands and reefs to head south, again, in order to end up in the middle of the West side. Considering Prince of Wales Island was a hundred and forty miles long and about sixty wide, that would entail a voyage that neither Lilly nor I—much less the *Glory B*—was up for, yet. None of us were in shape to hobble along much farther without some serious rest and refurbishing.

Our only option was to backtrack south to the hidden town of Thorne Bay we had not been able to locate, earlier, and inch our way around those little islands, rocks, and reefs that had seemed so foreboding to us before. And the sooner we got there, the better. I would wait only for a good weather forecast on the Clarance, then leave early enough to avoid the afternoon winds and chop. With Lilly up forward to keep a lookout for rocks and shallow places...

How hard could it be?

LOG OF THE GLORY B.
Ketchikan to Thorne Bay
2014

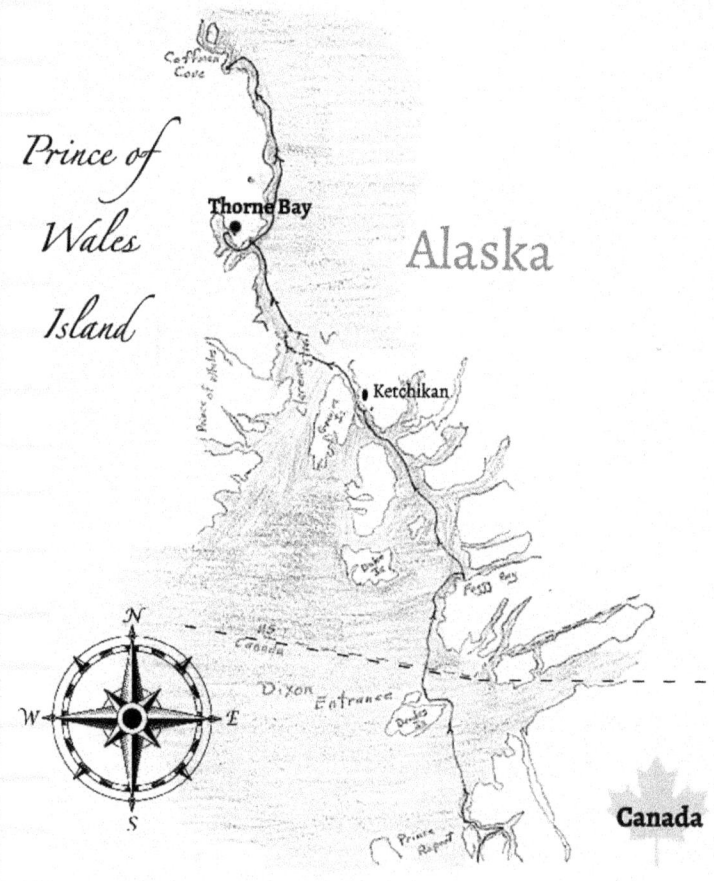

55.69° N   132.52° W

17 To See the Dream

Of course, I called ahead to the marina to make sure there would be a place for us there. I connected directly to the Harbor Master, and within a few minutes discovered that not only was there room for us, but they did have a real grocery store, and metered electricity along with a reasonable monthly fee. He was very personable and when I told him my wife was a writer and would need Internet access, he assured me there was Wifi at the library less than a block away. To top it off, he mentioned that his wife was a writer, as well, and had a book published, also.

Already, I could sense "God's footprints" ahead of us, leading the way in even this small setback of having to retrace our last few hours of our long journey. The whole trip had been a changing of our way of doing things differently than we had ever experienced before. In the beginning we had just struck out, much of the time not knowing what was ahead of us. Subconsciously, I found myself constantly on the alert for the next emergency. It wasn't until the prospect of finally getting to a place where we could slow down, catch our breath, and take account of where we could go from here that I realized how tired I was.

We needed to wake up in the same place for a while.

As unenthusiastic as we were about making another long run so soon—especially one going backwards—the trip turned out to be a beautiful one. We were going south, so the prevailing winds would be behind us if they came up, and we would at least not have to be beating into it at the end of the day. We could also raise the sails if necessary and actually do some sailing then, which seemed to make the boat more stable than just motoring along. After all, that's what sailboats were designed for: to work with the wind and waves rather than against them.

Retracing such a recent route took all the uncertainty out of constantly wondering where we were. I enjoyed recognizing places like Ratz Harbor and Forss Cove without having to search so intensely for the small characteristics that would assure me I was on the right track. Even the entrance to Thorne Bay was easier to see, knowing exactly how far it was from Snug Anchorage that we had so enjoyed.

It didn't seem as foreboding as it had before, due mostly to the difference in the tides. Being at a higher point this time, many of the rocks and "pinched channels" looked to have much more space than that first day we had inched around and through the narrow places. I saw Snug Anchorage—right where it should be—but passed it on by.

We were on a mission to find the town of Thorne Bay. The channel entrance marker was easy to identify and there was plenty of room to get past it. Being red, we kept it on our right to adhere to the old sailor's adage of "red, right, returning." Once through the winding entrance, everything seemed protected from the churning outside waters. Suddenly, all was peaceful.

As the bay widened out and the forested land rose up on both sides, we came in view of our first glimpse of civilization: a two-story float house, with a beautiful ketch tied up beside it. Surrounded by the spectacular beauty of nature, it was clearly the best of both worlds in the same spot. As I was drinking in the amazing image, Lilly commented that it would be "heaven on earth" to live in a place like that, and I agreed.

Not long after that, there were more of these float houses dotted in front of the shores, each set back in one of the many bays and coves that continued to unfold along the way. Then, came a house or two, onshore, then another and another. Some were quite large, with wide clearings where the dense trees had been cut back: obviously more of the many lodging establishments that were so numerous to the sport fishing industry. Finally the bay widened out to reveal two marinas: one smaller, on the South side, and—in the distance—another larger one set in the middle of what was clearly a neighborhood of homes and buildings on the North.

With total relief we headed toward the transient area which looked easily accessible, with plenty of open space for us to pull up to.

Normally, we would have taken care of the marina business, first. But coming so soon from a situation of not making sure a place actually had everything we would need there, it seemed more important to find out if this "real grocery store" truly had any fresh food in it. We had gone for many weeks on a diet of canned and dry goods from our own supplies with only the occasional bit of fresh produce that was always gone within a few days. Considering those places were few and far between in such a vast wilderness as the Tongass National Forest, there weren't many of those.

From where we stood, we could see no buildings that identified what we considered a town. Nothing that looked like a store or post office. There was a church in the middle, and farther on, some large metal buildings at the end but after that, the forest seemed crowded down to the waterfront, again. What we were looking for was probably tucked away somewhere inland and we would have to ask directions.

The docks we walked along held the now familiar, covered fish-cleaning station at one end and rows of slips occupied mostly by commercial and sport fishing boats. There was a long ramp leading up to the marina office and the road, and we were told the grocery store was just around the corner, a short distance away, at the end of the street where it curved to continue on into a waterfront residential area.

The road was lined on both sides with a variety of small homes crowded together that ranged from cabins, mobile homes, and several larger custom homes. They faced a stream that was so full of huge salmon making their way in from the bay we could see their fins churning the water as we walked along.

Then—where the road turned to cross a wooden bridge over the stream before heading up the hill on the other side—was the welcome site of a building with cars parked in front of it. There was an ice machine and even a neat row of shopping baskets outside the door. We had arrived. And the short walk had taken less than ten minutes.

As Lilly headed away, immediately, to explore every isle, I fell into my typical custom of hanging out at the front to chat with locals. The cashiers were pleasantly talkative and friendly, beyond the customary "Hello," and "Have a nice day." I realized there was the possibility that I could strike up a conversation which I could actually get some information from. Even though it was the height of the summer season and people were coming and going, everyone was relaxed and comfortable enough to join in on any conversation within hearing distance of the two check-out areas.

No hurries. I quickly recognized that this was an important hub of the town and part of the shopping experience was visiting with whoever was there. It was our first personal encounter with the island culture. As pleasant as it was, I realized it had been a while since I had seen Lilly and the store wasn't that big. So, I meandered past the ends of the isles to see if she needed help with anything. It was only a moment before I was at the end of the front corner in the produce section and I hadn't found her. There was nowhere to disappear to, so I stood there, knowing she should end up in this spot, sooner or later.

As I waited, an elderly lady came down the isle pushing a cart with a young girl hanging onto it. The elementary teacher in me kicked in and I made some comment about shopping with Grandma, today.

The woman gave me a friendly smile and introduced the child before telling me, "All the children call me, Gram, here."

There was an immediate connection between us. Here was a woman who loved children as much as I did. About that time, Lilly showed up from the other direction and I introduced the two of them, adding that we had just arrived in town less than an hour, ago, and were enjoying their real grocery store.

"It's the best one on the island," she replied. "If you want something special they don't have, they'll make sure it's on the next order, and keep it stocked if it's a brand you use all the time."

We were in paradise. Then followed a few of the questions people always asked about us: where and how we got there, which was feeling pretty humdrum to us by now, and certainly nothing spectacular. So, I gave her the shortest version.

"You should come for coffee, tomorrow, and tell me more about it."

We must have hesitated, wondering if we had heard her right.

"I only live right up the hill," she assured. "Just a short walk from here."

"What's the address?" I asked.

"Oh, you can't miss it. The gray house, the biggest one on the hill."

"What time?" Lilly wanted to know.

"Whenever you would like. I'm up and have the coffee on anytime after seven-thirty." Then she headed off with smile.

We stood there for a moment in silence before I

commented, "She sure was friendly."

"Do you think she really meant it? Anytime after seven-thirty? We're perfect strangers."

"She must or she wouldn't have invited us."

"We better go then."

It was a beautiful walk to her house the next morning. So much that we had to stop on the bridge for a while just to watch the hoards of salmon churning the waters as they struggled upstream. Once across, there was a bench facing out on the sea side, shaded by the giant trees that lined the shore: obviously a favorite spot to sit and enjoy the amazing view.

Farther along, the shore side of the hill was lined with heavily-ladened blackberry bushes that were too tempting to pass by without tasting. Delicious! A few minutes later, we passed only a couple houses before finding ourselves standing on a wide wooden deck lined with numerous flower pots, and a porch that led up to the door. There was a sign on it that said, "Welcome, come on in!"

I knocked, then cautiously opened the door and stuck my head in. There was Gram, sitting in a comfortable chair at the corner of a large living room, against a bank of windows that showcased the bay. From there, you could not only see boats coming and going, but also the float planes that took off and landed several times a day to deliver or take away island visitors.

The smell of fresh-brewed coffee and homemade banana bread was wonderful. She got up, with her pleasant smile and invited us to a small round table where the goodies were laid out, and told us to help ourselves. It felt like "coming home to family" there. The living area was open, with a kitchen at one end, that faced out onto a covered deck with more small tables and hanging flower baskets. It seemed like a place specifically set up to accommodate large numbers of people to gather and visit in. Later, we found out that's exactly what it was: designed by Gram, herself, and beautifully decorated with antiques that had been collected over a lifetime.

We had over an hour of pleasant conversation, in which we quickly discovered that she was not only a fellow Christian but had been responsible for the building of the church we had noticed. More than that, she had gone beyond the physical structure and was dedicated to sharing the love and "good news" of Jesus, with anyone and everyone she met. Truly, she was a kindred spirit.

Before we knew it, we were sharing much more than the brief description of our trip of a lifetime. We were telling how it had been the fulfillment of a long-ago dream we had thought to be lost, that—while it had been full of mishaps and mistakes—it had also been overflowing with miracles. The presence of God had accompanied us all the way.

To which her response was, "What can I do for you?"

For many years, we had been resolved to do all we could to spread the "good news," ourselves, but no one had ever encouraged us. Much less, offered to help or get involved in any of the things that we had so strongly in our hearts. So I didn't know quite how to respond to that, other than to say we were in need of some rest and recuperation time, not only for us but to take care of the major things I had put off on the *Glory B.* I was concerned for Lilly, as well. She needed to catch up on her deadlines, and resolve the problems incurred by the loss of her computer.

But, as for what we were going to do after that... I didn't know.

What was I doing here?

Looking back on it, I realized everything I had

believed for in Oklahoma had been fulfilled way beyond our wildest expectations. Not only did we possess the boat of our dreams, we were literally standing in a paradise we hadn't even known existed before. We had come all the way to Alaska. Our trip of a lifetime was over, and yet...

What comes after this?

Neither Lilly or I were ready to go home, yet. For one thing, we had barely touched the edge of this fascinating wilderness area made up of hundreds of islands and dotted with small communities that we had been drawn to for so many years. I at least wanted to visit the towns we had started out for. There was also the fact that our home still had other people living in it at the moment. By the end of our first day in Thorne Bay, we knew beyond a doubt we were in the perfect spot to rest, do repairs, and count up our resources before going on. And yet...

Something had happened to us out here. Somehow, in stepping out and acting on what we believed, we had become different people than we were when we started out. It had happened gradually, the same way learning the ways of the sea had come to us. By personally venturing out into it one step at a time. God had met us at every turn, bailed us out of many foolish situations we had made for ourselves. Yet, He had been with us all the way. And because of this, I did not want to go back to the way things were before. I had never felt so vibrant and alive, or filled with such confidence as I had been on this journey.

I did not want to lose that.

Somewhere in my life I had barreled past the in-depth stuff of where my heart was going. While I don't know exactly how that happened, I knew I did not want it to happen, again. Now, I was beginning to see that my effort to grab hold of a single scripture from my stack of cards had turned into a life-changing experience. My part had been taking the first step and seeing how far I could go to prove that promise true.

Very few times along the way did I know what lay farther ahead of us than the next anchorage. We were simply "on our way to Alaska." But there was a sort of freedom in that. I no longer had any doubts about where I was going or that I might not make it there. I had a feeling that it was only the beginning and that—if I wanted to—I could go anywhere I wanted. What else did I want? Before we came here, I had no idea such an island existed outside of the stuff of dreams. Yet, here was the physical evidence that it did.

In the beginning I knew that I could not do this on my own. Not at my age. Yet, here I was, feeling better than I had ever felt in my life. Getting a classic sailboat had been a life's dream. Miraculously getting the exact make and model I had yearned so much for thirty years earlier made me believe I could go one step further and go somewhere in it.

Could other things be waiting for us somewhere out here, as the *Glory B* had waited for us all those years: something tailored especially for us—a mission that no one else could fulfill but was still an option if we were only brave enough to give it one more shot? By faith, this time—in partnership—with the Lord in control, and not trying to do everything all on our own? Years ago, Lilly and I had wanted to have an "island ministry," but we let something we called "real life" get in the way until it seemed like too late. Maybe this "trip of a lifetime" would have to suffice.

Or would it?

Wonderful things were calling to me here: a glorious mixture of my past and present that seemed to be coming to life all over, again. What if there

Glory B!

actually was something more? What if that long ago dream was already here and waiting? I'm not sure where it is but I know exactly what it will look like. I only have to start looking for it.

One step at a time.

*"I tell you...whatever you ask in prayer,
believe that you have received it,
and it will be yours."*

Mark 11:24

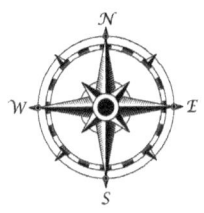

A Note To Readers

Thanks for going along on this journey with me. In looking back, I am reminded most of how important that daily compass setting turned out to be. The few times I disregarded it were disastrous. I was so sure I knew where I was. But how deceiving what we see with our eyes can be! And how faithful it was to lead me in the right direction even in a fog.

As long as I believed it.

No alarm ever went off to caution me I was making a mistake, or straying too far off the path. The little needle simply continued to point quietly and steadily in the right direction. I have found that to be true in more than just sailing.

All of life is a journey, really. And—who knows—maybe our heart has a compass all its own. Especially when we stay in the same place for too long, or get that uncomfortable feeling there's somewhere else we should be. Not only would my difficulties have been reduced if I had paid more attention, but I'm convinced that's how I ended up at seventy without having done so many of the things I truly wanted to do.

Even though I made a lot of mistakes on this trip —from simply embarrassing to literally life and death situations—I wouldn't trade the experience for anything. It changed me in ways I had been disappointed about for a long time. More importantly, it convinced me there really was something better for me out here, if only I would take a step out of my comfort zone and look for it.

It is my prayer that this book will encourage others to do the same.

Dave Graham
Thorne Bay, Alaska

About the Author

Having traveled twice around the world during his Navy years, Dave Graham had a love for the sea that he could see stretching all the way back to his Danish ancestors. He owned several boats—not counting the small stuff like dinghies or canoes that he built, himself—throughout his career as an educator and work in the behavioral sciences for troubled youth.

When the near-forgotten dream of making a long voyage in a deep water sailboat pulled him out of retirement, he realized he still had resources inside that he had never tapped into. That journey led to things much bigger than he dreamed.

You can get in touch with him on his Website over at:

CaptainGloryB.com

This Book was published by:

If you enjoyed it, please consider leaving a review in any of the places you like to buy books. To browse other books like this—both fiction and nonfiction—visit:

LightsmithPublishers.com

We appreciate you taking the time to read! We hope you will take advantage of our FREE EBOOKS that are new each month.

Lilly Maytree has been writing books and adventuring with her captain husband aboard the sailing ketch *Glory B* for a long time. The *Stella Madison Capers* were originally written during their long voyage up the Inside Passage to Alaska, along the same route that her fictional characters followed.

It also includes a very brief account of her own true-life "trip of a lifetime" from her point of view. Which is sometimes necessary. Although there were many similarities between the true story and the imagined one, the Captain and Lilly ended up on a beautiful island in Southeast Alaska. They loved it so much they never went home.

You can find out more about Lilly
and her books by visiting:

LillyMaytree.com

Are there any children in your life?
You might enjoy a visit to:

Books that range from **Early Readers through Young Adult**, and home of the

Wilderness Kids Club

FREE eBook offer each month!

www.ingramcontent.com/pod-product-compliance
Lightning Source LLC
Chambersburg PA
CBHW041126110526
44592CB00020B/2706